Hamoodur Rahman Commission
Supplementary Report

as Released by
The Government of Pakistan

ISBN: 978-1-60450-020-2

Library of Congress Cataloging-in-Publication Data

Pakistan. Hamoodur Rehman Commission of Inquiry into the 1971 War.

Hamoodur Rahman Commission : supplementary report / Government of Pakistan 1974.

p. cm.

ISBN 978-1-60450-020-2 (alk. paper)

1. India-Pakistan Conflict, 1971. 2. Bangladesh--History--Revolution, 1971. 3. Pakistan--Politics and government. I. Title.

DS388.P33 2007

954.9205'1--dc22

2007033133

Published by Arc Manor
P. O. Box 10339
Rockville, MD 20849-0339

Printed in the United States of America

Hamoodur Rahman Commission of Inquiry into the 1971 India-Pakistan War, Supplementary Report

ARC
MANOR
Rockville, Maryland
2007

Contents

INTRODUCTION

REASONS FOR SUPPLEMENTARY REPORT

This commission of Inquiry was appointed by the President of Pakistan in December, 1971 to inquire into and find out "the circumstances in which the Commander, Eastern command, surrendered and the members of the Armed Forces of Pakistan under his command laid down their arms and a cease-fire was ordered along the borders of West Pakistan and India and along the cease-fire line in the State of Jammu and Kashmir." After having examined 213 witnesses the Commission submitted its report in July 1972.

2. Before we submitted that report of necessity we did not have the evidence of most of the persons taken as prisoners of war, including the major personalities, who played a part in the final events culminating in the surrender in East Pakistan with the exception only of Major General Rahim. Although we did our best to reconstruct the East Pakistan story with the help of such material, as was then available, inevitably our conclusions had to be of a tentative character. We also felt that since we had found rea-

sons adversely to comment upon the performance of some of the major figures involved it would have been unfair to pass any final judgment upon them without giving them an opportunity of explaining their own view point. For this reason we said that "our observations and conclusions regarding the surrender in East Pakistan and other allied matters should be regarded as provisional and subject to modification in the light of the evidence of the Commander, Eastern Command, and his senior officers as and when such evidence becomes available." (Page 242 of the Main Report).

Commission Reactivated

3. Accordingly, after the prisoners of war and the civil personnel who had also been interned with the military personnel in India returned to Pakistan, the Federal government issued a notification directing "that the Commission shall start inquiry at a place and on a date to be fixed by it and complete the inquiry and submit its report to the President of Pakistan, with its findings as to the matters aforesaid, within a period of two months commencing from the date the commission starts functioning." A copy of this notification is annexed as Annexure A to this Chapter. Lt. Gen. (Retd.) Altaf Qadir, who had also previously acted as Military Adviser to the Commission, was re-appointed as such as also was Mr. M.A Latif as Secretary to the Commission. At the request of the commission the government also appointed Col. M.A Hassan as Legal Advisor.

4. The commission issued a Press Release on the 1st June, 1974 offering an opportunity to the prisoners of War and others repatriated from East Pakistan to furnish such information as might be within their knowledge and relevant to the purposes of the Commission. A copy of this Press Release is in Annexure B to this Chapter.

8

5. Commission held an informal meeting at Lahore on the 3rd June, 1974 to consider various preliminary matters and then decided to resume proceedings at Abbottabad from the 16th July, 1974. In the meantime a number of questionnaires were issued to various persons, including those who were at the helm of affairs in East Pakistan, at the relevant time and others whom we considered likely to have relevant knowledge. Statements were also sent from members of armed forces, civil services and the police services involved and we then proceeded after scrutiny of these statements to summon the witnesses.

We recorded evidence of as many as 72 persons and these included particularly Lt. Gen. A.A.K. Niazi, Commander Eastern Command, Major Generals Farman Ali, Jamshed ad the generals who held during the relevant time commands of divisions, Rear Admiral Sharif, who was the senior most Naval Officer, Air Commodore Inam the senior most Air Officer, and civilian personnel, including the then Chief Secretary Mr. Muzaffar Hussain and the Inspector General of Police Mr. Mahmood Ali Chaudhry. Besides, Maj. Gen. Rahim was reexamined. The only exception which was unavoidable was that Dr. Malik who till very nearly the end was the Governor of East Pakistan, but in his case also we had firsthand evidence of every important event and we, therefore, now feel ourselves competent to submit our final conclusions.

6. After the examination of evidence the Commission, finding itself unable to submit its report for a number of reasons by the 15th of September 1974, asked for time which was extended till the 15th of November 1974 and again till the 30th November 1974. At the conclusion of the recording of evidence on the 5th September 1974 we had to disperse principally because two of us were required to attend the special session of the Supreme Court

at Karachi from the 9th to the 21st September, 1974 and the President had also to proceeded to Geneva to attend an International Conference. We, therefore, reassembled on the 23rd of October, 1974 at Abbottabad to prepare this Supplement to our main report.

SCHEME OF THE SUPPLEMENTARY REPORT

7. In general although we have examined a considerable volume of fresh evidence we have found no reason whatever to modify the conclusions that we reached and stated in the Main Report; if anything by reasons of more detailed information we are confirmed in those conclusions. We, therefore, propose to avoid a repetition of what we stated in the Main Report except to some slight degree necessary for restating briefly some of the conclusions with which we are principally concerned in this supplement.

There are also some matters upon which our information was then scanty if not negligible and, these we, therefore, propose to deal with in some detail. We do, however, propose to write this, supplement, following the same pattern as far as is practicable, as we did in the main report. In Part II of that report we dealt with the political background and to this we now intend to add only matters which occurred in 1971, or to be more specific on and after the 25th March, 1971. We have nothing to add to Part III of the Main Report dealing with International Relations. As to Part IV we propose to say nothing in regard to the military aspect in so far as it concerned West Pakistan except to a limited extent as to its repercussions in East Pakistan and as to some controversy that has been raised before us as to the wisdom of opening the Western Front at all.

Of necessity in this part, however, we shall deal in greater detail with the matters dealt with in Chapters II, III, IV, V, VI, VII, VIII and IX of the Main Report in so far as they concern East Pakistan. We then propose to deal with the subject of discipline of the armed forces in East Pakistan which would include the questions of alleged military atrocities in East Pakistan. We shall of necessity, mainly in this part, have to deal with the individual conduct of several persons though aspects of this will emerge from earlier Chapters. We shall then need to discuss some evidence which has come before us suggesting that there were, during the period of captivity in India, concerted efforts on the part of some high officers to present a consistent, if it necessarily accurate, account of what took place. We propose finally to wind up this supplement by making the recommendations

CABINET NOTE

Government of Pakistan

Cabinet Secretary
(Cabinet Division)
Rawalpindi, the 25th May, 1974

No. 107/19/74-Min -Whereas the Commission of Inquiry appointed under the late Ministry of Presidential Affairs Notification No. 632 (1)/71, dated the 26th December, 1971, had, in its report of 8th July, 1972, submitted, inter alia, that the Commission's findings with regard to the courses of events in East Pakistan were only tentative and recommended that "as and when the Commander Eastern Command and other senior officers now prisoners of war in India are available, a further Inquiry should be held into the circumstances which led to the surrender in East Pakistan";

And whereas all the prisoners of war and civil internees have now returned to Pakistan;

And whereas the Federal Government is of the opinion that it is necessary in the light of the recommendations of the Commission of Inquiry to finalise the said inquiry as to the circumstances which led to the surrender in East Pakistan, after examining any of the said prisoners of war and civil internees whose examination is considered necessary by the Commission;

Now, therefore, in exercise of the powers conferred by sub-section (I) of Section 30 the Pakistan Commissions of Inquiry Act, 1956 (VI of 1956) the federal government is pleased to direct that the commission shall start inquiry at a place and on a date to be fixed by it and complete the inquiry and submit its report to the President of Pakistan, with its findings as to the matter aforesaid, within a period of two months commencing from the date the Commission starts functioning.

Sd/

Vaqar Ahmad

Cabinet Secretary.

Lahore, the 1st June, 1974

Press Release

The War Inquiry Commission which has been asked by the government of Pakistan to resume its deliberations and submit a final report was appointed by the then President of Pakistan, Mr. Zulfikar Ali Bhutto, on the 26th December, 1971 to enquire into the circumstances in which the Commander, Eastern Command surrendered and the members of the armed forces of Pakistan under his command laid down their arms and a cease-fire was ordered along the borders of West Pakistan and India and along the cease-fire line in the State of Jammu and Kashmir. The Commission is headed by the Chief Justice of Pakistan, Mr. Justice Hamoodur Rahman. The other two members of the Commission are Mr. Justice S. Anwarul Haq, Judge, Supreme Court of Pakistan and Mr. Justice Tufaif Ali Abdur Rahman, Chief Justice of Sid and Baluchistan High Court. Lt. Gen (Rtd) Altaf Qadir and Mr. M.A Latif, Assistant Registrar of the Supreme Court of Pakistan are Military Adviser and Secretary of the Commission, respectively.

The Commission which had started its proceedings in camera in Rawalpindi on the 1st February, 1972 recorded evidence of 213 witnesses. It had submitted its report to the then President of Pakistan on the 12th July, 1972. In the Report the Commission had observed that its findings with regard to the causes of surrender in East Pakistan were only tentative. It, therefore, recommended that as and when the Commander, Eastern Command and other senior officers who were in India at that time were available, a further inquiry should be held into the circumstances which led to the surrender in East Pakistan. Now that all the prisoners of war and civil internees have returned to Pakistan, the Government has asked the Commission to complete this part of its inquiry.

A temporary office of the Commission has been set up for the present in the Supreme Court building at Lahore and the Commission has decided that before commencing its proceeding a place to be announced later on the members of the public civil services and the armed forces who were either prisoners of war in India or were otherwise repatriated from East Pakistan should be given an opportunity to furnish to the commission such relevant information as may be within their knowledge relating to the causes of surrender in East Pakistan. This information should be submitted in writing, preferably 5 copies, as briefly as possible by the 30th June, 1974 at the latest to the Secretary of the Inquiry Commission care of Supreme Court of Pakistan, Lahore. The informant should also state whether he will be willing to appear before the Commission.

All such information and particulars of the persons given the information will be strictly confidential. It may be mentioned that according to a public announcement of the Government of Pakistan published in newspapers on the 11th January, 1972 all proceedings before the Commission would be in camera and the statements made before and addressed to it would be absolutely privileged and would not render a person making any such statement liable to any civil or criminal proceedings except when such statement is false. The Commission is empowered to call before it any citizen of Pakistan to seek information. The Commission can if necessary even issue warrants to secure the attendance of any person unless he is otherwise exempted by law from personal appearance before a Court. The serving personnel of defence services who are willing to give evidence before the Commission should have no apprehension of victimization for assisting the Commission in its task.

CHAPTER 1
THE MORAL ASPECT

INTRODUCTORY

In Chapter I of Part V of the Main Report, we have dealt at some length with the moral aspect of the causes of our defeat in the 1971 War. This became necessary in view of the vehement assertions made before the Commission by a large number of respectable witnesses drawn from various sections of society, including highly placed and responsible Service Officers, to the effect that due to corruption arising out of the performance of Martial Law duties, lust for wine and women and greed for lands and houses, a large number of senior Army Officers, particularly those occupying the highest positions, had not only lost the will to fight but also the professional competence necessary for taking the vital and critical decisions demanded of them for the successful prosecution of the war. It was asserted by these witnesses that men given to a disreputable way of life could hardly be expected to lead the Pakistan Army to victory.

2. After analysing the evidence brought before the Commission, we came to the conclusion that the process of moral degeneration among the senior ranks of the Armed Forces was set in motion by their involvement in Martial Law duties in 1958, that these tendencies reappeared and were, in fact, intensified when Martial Law was imposed in the country once again in March 1969 by General Yahya Khan, and that there was indeed substance in the allegations that a considerable number of senior Army Officers had not only indulged in large scale acquisition of lands and houses and other commercial activities, but had also adopted highly immoral and licentious ways of life which seriously affected their professional capabilities and their qualities of leadership.

3. We then offered specific comments on the conduct of certain high officers including the Commander, Eastern Command, Lt. Gen A.A.K. Niazi. However, we observed, in Paragraph 35 of that Chapter, that "as we have not had the opportunity of putting these allegations to Lt. Gen. A.A.K. Niazi any finding in this behalf must await his return from India where he is at present held as a prisoner of war". We have now examined not only Lt. Gen. Niazi but certain other witnesses as well in relation to his personal conduct, and the general allegations made against the Pakistan Army during its operations in the former East Pakistan, and are accordingly in a position to formulate our final conclusions in the matter.

EFFECT OF MARTIAL LAW DUTIES

4. In the situation that developed after the military action of the 25th of March 1971, the civil administration in East Pakistan practically came to a standstill, and the burden of running the Province fell heavily upon the Army Officers. Their involvement in civil administration continued unabated even after the induction of a sizable number of

senior civil servants from West Pakistan, including the Chief Secretary, the Inspector General of Police and at least two Division Commissioners.

5. According to the Inspector General of Police, Mr. M.A.K Chaudhry (Witness No. 219), "after the disturbances of March-April 1971, there was a Military Governor with a Major General as his adviser at the head of the civil administration. There was a parallel Martial Law administration at all levels. All wings of administration, relating to law and order were under the control of Martial Law Authorities. A West Pakistan Deputy Inspector General of Police in the field was not permitted by the local Martial Law Authorities to come to the Provincial Headquarters" for a conference with the Inspector General of Police. In the view of Syed Alamdar Raza (Witness No. 226), Commissioner of Dacca Division, "efforts were made to make civilian officers responsible or at least routine matters within the general supervision and control of the Army Officers, but no substantial results could be achieved. Those Bengali Officers who had been restored lacked confidence and were not sure if their loyalties were not suspected. Action was taken against them, even their arrests were ordered without any body knowing about it, including their superiors or the Government of East Pakistan."

6. The Army's involvement in civil administration did not come to an end even with the installation of a civilian governor (viz. Dr. A.M Malik), and the ministers appointed by him. The observations made in this behalf by Maj Gen. Rao Farman Ali (Witness No. 284), who held the appointment of Maj General (Civil Affairs) in the governor's Secretariat are worth quoting:

"A fully civil government could not be formed in East Pakistan as had been announced by the ex-President. Dr. Malik an old man and politician, had a weak personality. He could not annoy, the Martial Law Administrator (Lt. Gen.

A.A.K. Niazi) also because of the unsettled conditions obtaining in the Wing. Gen Niazi, on the other hand, cherished and liked power, but did not have the breadth of vision or ability to understand political implications. He did not display much respect for the civilian Governor,..... The Army virtually continued to control civil administration".

7. The impression created on the mind of the West Pakistani civilian officials, then serving in East Pakistan, has been stated thus by Mr. Mohammad Ashraf, (Witness No. 275), former Additional Deputy Commissioner, Dacca: "The installation of a civilian governor in September 1971 was merely to hoodwink public opinion at home and abroad. Poor Dr. Malik and his ministers were figureheads only. Real decisions in all important matters still lay with the Army. I remember the first picture of the new Cabinet. Maj. Gen Farman Ali was prominently visible sitting on the right side of the Governor, although he was not a member of the Cabinet."

8. This impression is fortified by the fact that at a later stage even the selection of candidates for the by-elections ordered by General Yahya Khan was made by Maj Gen Farman Ali. Lt. Gen Niazi and some of his subordinate Martial Law Administrators have no doubt claimed that they allowed full liberty of action to the civilian officials at various levels, but even they have conceded that in the peculiar situation prevailing in East Pakistan after the military action the Army necessarily continued to be deeply concerned with the maintenance of law and order, the restoration of communications and the revival of economic activity in the Province.

9. The evidence of Officers repatriated from India leaves no doubt that this extensive and prolonged involvement of the Pakistan Army in Martial Law duties and civil administration had a disastrous effect on its professional and moral standards. According to Brig. M. Saleemullah, who

was commanding 203 (A) Brigade in East Pakistan, "prolonged commitment on Martial Law duties and interment security roles had affected the professional standards of the Army." According to Rear Admiral M. Sharif (Witness No. 283) who was the Flag Officer Commanding the Pakistan Navy in East Pakistan, "the foundation of this defeat was laid way back in 1958 when the Armed Forces took over the country ..." While learning the art of politics in this newly assigned role to themselves, they gradually abandoned their primary function of the art of soldiering, they also started amassing wealth and usurping status for themselves. Similar views were expressed before us by Commodore I.H. Malik (Witness No. 272) who was the Chairman of the Chittagong Port Trust until the day of surrender, Brigadier S.S.A Qasim, former Commander Artillery, Eastern Command, Col. Mansoorul Haw Malik, former GS-I, 9 division, East Pakistan, and Col. Ijaz Ahmad (Witness No. 247) former Colonel Staff (GS) Eastern Command, to mention only a few.

10. The fresh evidence coming before the Commission has thus served only to reinforce the conclusions reached by us in the Main Report that the involvement of the Pakistan Army in Martial Law duties and civil administration had a highly corrupting influence, seriously detracting from the professional duties of the Army and affecting the quality of training which the Officers could impart to their units and formations, for the obvious reason that they did not have enough time available for this purpose, and many of them also lost the inclination to do so.

LIVING OFF THE LAND

11. A new aggravating factor made its appearance in East Pakistan in the wake of the military action of the 25th of March 1971, when units of the Pakistan Army undertook "sweep operations" throughout the Province to deal with

the Awami League insurgents. The Army had to go out into the countryside without adequate logistic arrangements, and was compelled, at least in the early stages of its operations to take its requirements of food-grains and other essential supplies from civilian sources. Unfortunately, however, the practice appears to have persisted even when it became possible to make proper logistic arrangements. There is evidence to the effect that civilian shops and stores were broken into by the troops without preparing any record of what was taken and from where. The need for commandeering vehicles, foodstuffs, medicines and other essential supplies can certainly be appreciated, but this should have been done under a proper method of accounting so that compensation could be paid on return of normal conditions. As no such procedure was adopted, it led to a general feeling among the troops, including their officers that they were entitled to take whatever they wanted from wherever they liked. This appears to us to be the genesis of the looting alleged to have been indulged in by the Army in East Pakistan.

12. In the early stages this method of procurement seems to have been encouraged by senior commanders, including Lt. Gen Niazi, whose remarks on the very first day of his taking over command from Lt. Gen Tikka Khan have already been quoted by us in an earlier chapter, viz: "what have I been hearing about shortage of rations? Are not there any cows and goats in this country? This is enemy territory. Get what you want. This is what we used to do in Burma." (vide Maj Gen Farman Ali's Evidence). Gen Niazi did not, of course, accept having made any such statement and asserted that "whatever we took we gave a chit so that civil government should pay for that." This assertion is not supported by other officers. On the contrary, some officers like Lt. Col. Bukhori, (Witness No. 244) have made a positive statement that even written orders were received

by them emanating from the Eastern Command to live of the land during sweep operations.

13. However, at a later stage the Eastern Command and the divisional Commanders issued strict instructions in an effort to stop such practices, and some Commanders caused searches to be carried out of the barracks occupied by the troops for the recovery of looted material which included television sets, refrigerators, typewriters, watches, gold, air conditioners and other attractive items. We were informed that in several cases disciplinary action by way of Courts of Inquiries was initiated but the cases could not be finalised for one reasons or the other before the surrender on the 16th of December 1971.

GLARING CASES OF MORAL LAPSES AMONGST OFFICERS POSTED IN EAST PAKISTAN

(1) Lt. Gen A.A.K. Niazi

14. In the Main Report we have mentioned the allegations, and the evidence relating thereto as regards the personal conduct of Gen. Yahya Khan, Gen. Abdul Hamid Khan the late Maj Gen (Retd) Khuda Dad Khan, Lt. Gen A.A.K. Niazi, Maj Gen. Jehanzeb and Brig Hayatullah. We wish to supplement those observations as regards Lt. Gen Niazi.

15. From a perusal of Paragraphs 30 to 34 of Chapter 1 of Part V of the Main Report, it will be seen that the graveness of the allegations made against Lt. Gen. Niazi is that he was making money in the handling of Martial Law cases while posted as G.O.C Sialkot and later as G.O.C and Martial Law Administrator at Lahore; that he was on intimate terms with one Mrs. Saeeda Bukhari of Gulberg, Lahore, who was running a brothel under the name of Senorita Home, and was also acting as the General's tout for receiving bribes and getting things done; that he

was also friendly with another woman called Shamini Firdaus of Sialkot who was said to be playing the same role as Mrs. Saeeda Bukhari of Lahore; that during his stay in East Pakistan he came to acquire a stinking reputation owing to his association with women of bad repute, and his nocturnal visits to places also frequented by several junior officers under his command; and that he indulged in the smuggling of Pan from East Pakistan to West Pakistan. These allegations were made before the Commission by Abdul Qayyum Arif (witness No. 6), Munawar Hussain, Advocate of Sialkot (Witness No. 13), Abdul Hafiz Kardar (Witness No. 25), Maj Sajjadul Haq (Witness No. 164), Squadron Leader C.A Wahid (Witness No. 57) and Lt. Col Haliz Ahmad (Witness NO. 147).

16. During the present phase of our inquiry damaging evidence has come on the record regarding the ill repute of General Niazi in sex matters, and his indulgence in the smuggling of Pan. A mention may be made in this behalf of the statements made before us by Lt. Col. Mansoorul Haq (Witness No. 260), ex GSO-I, 9 div. Lt Cdr. A.A. Khan (Witness No. 262), of Pakistan navy, Brig I.R Shariff (Witness No. 269) former Comd. Engrs. Eastern Command, Mr. Mohammad Ashraf (Witness No. 275) former Addl. D.C. Dacca, and Lt. Col. Aziz Ahmad Khan (Witness No. 276). The remarks made by this last witness are highly significant: "The troops used to say that when the Commander (Lt. Gen. Niazi) was himself a raper, how could they be stopped. Gen. Niazi enjoyed the same reputation at Sialkot and Lahore."

17. Maj Gen Qazi Abdul Majid Khan (Witness No. 254) and Maj Gen. Farman Ali (Witness No. 284) have also spoken of Gen Niazi's indulgence in the export of Pan. According to Maj Gen Abdul Majid, Brig Aslam Niazi, commanding 53 Bde, and Senior Superintendent of Police Diljan, who was residing with Gen. Niazi in the Flag Staff House at Dacca, were helping Gen Niazi in the export of Pan. Maj.

Gen. Farman Ali has gone to the extent of stating that "Gen Niazi was annoyed with me because I had not helped him in Pan business. Brig Hamiduddin of PIA had complained to me that Corps Headquarter was interfering in transportation of Pan to West Pakistan by placing limitation on poundage. I told ADC to Gen. Niazi, who visited me in my office, that this was a commercial matter and should be left to the arrangements arrived at between PIA and Pan exporters." We understand that the insinuation is that a son of Gen. Niazi was engaged in the export of Pan from East Pakistan to West Pakistan. According to Major S.S. Haider (Witness NO. 259) and Brig Atta Mohammed (Witness No. 257) even Brig Baqir Siddiqui, Chief of Staff, Eastern Command, was a partner of Gen Niazi in the export of Pan.

18. The allegations mentioned in the preceding Paragraphs were put to Lt. Gen. Niazi during his appearance before us, and he naturally denied them. When asked about his weakness for the fair sex, he replied, "I say no. I have been doing Martial Law duties. I never stopped anybody coming to see me. I became very religious during the East Pakistan trouble. I was not so before. I thought more of death than these things."

19. As regards the allegation that he was indulging in the export of Pan, he stated that he had ordered an enquiry into the matter on the complaint of a man called Bhuiyan who was aggrieved by the monopoly position occupied by the Pan exporters. He alleged that in fact Brig Hamiduddin and PIA staff were themselves involved in the smuggling of Pan.

20. From the mass of evidence coming before the Commission from witnesses, both civil and military, there is little doubt that Gen. Niazi unfortunately came to acquire a bad reputation in sex matters, and this reputation has been consistent during his postings in Sialkot, Lahore and

East Pakistan. The allegations regarding his indulgence in the export of Pan by using or abusing his position in the Eastern Command and as Zonal Martial Law Administrator also prima facie appear to be well-founded, although it was not our function to hold a detailed inquiry into the matter. It is for the Government to decide whether these matters should also form the subject of any inquiry or trial which may have to be ultimately held against this officer.

(2) MAJ GEN MOHAMMAD JAMSHED, FORMER GOC 36 (A) DIVISION, EAST PAKISTAN

21. Col. Bashir Ahmad Khan (Witness No. 263) who was posted as DDML, Eastern Command, stated before the Commission that the wife of Maj Gen Jamshed Khan had brought some currency with her while being evacuated from Dacca on the morning of 16th of December 1971. He further alleged that Lt. Col Rashid, Col. Staff of the East Pakistan Civil Armed Forces, commanded by Maj Gen. Jamshed Khan, was also reported to have been involved in the misappropriation of currency. It further came to our notice that the General had distributed some money among persons who left East Pakistan by helicopters on the morning of 15th or 16th of December 1971.

22. An inquiry was made from Maj Gen. Jamshed Khan in this behalf, and his reply is as under. :

The total sum involved was Rs. 50,000 which I had ordered to be drawn from the currency that was being destroyed under Government instructions and the total amount was distributed by the officers detailed by me and strictly according to the instruction/rules and regulations to the Binaries and Bengalis, informers, and to the needy on night 15/16th December 1971.

A secret fund was placed at my disposal by the Government of East Pakistan for the purpose of payment of rewards and purchase of information and in this case the expenditure was from the secret fund at my disposal. This fund was non-auditable. The money given to the needy families who were dispatched by helicopters on night 15th/16th December, 1971 was from the EPCAF Director General's Fund. I was the sole authority to sanction from this fund and considering the circumstances under which this expenditure was made I had no intention to recommend recovery from persons concerned.

From the above clarification it will be appreciated that there was no requirement to furnish details of the above expenditure to any accounts department."

23. We regret we cannot regard the reply given by Maj. Gen. Jamshed as satisfactory. Even though the funds disbursed by him may not be auditable in ordinary circumstances, it would have been appropriate and advisable for him to supply such information as was possible for him to do in the circumstances once the question of the disposal of these funds had arisen on the basis of information supplied to the Commission by officers who heard of these transactions in East Pakistan and later in the prisoners of war camps. We suggest, therefore, without necessarily implying any dereliction on the part of the general, that the matter should be inquired into further so that the suspicion surrounding the same is cleared in the General's own interest.

(3) Brig. Jehanzeb Arbab, former Commander 57 Brigade.

(4) Lt. Col. (Now Brig) Muzaffar Ali Khan Zahid, former CO 31 field Regiment.

(5) Lt. Col. Basharat Ahmad, former CO 18 Punjab

(6) Lt. Col. Mohammad Taj, CO 32 Punjab

(7) Lt. Col Mohammad Tufail, Col 55 Field Regiment

(8) Major Madad Hussain Shah, 18 Punjab

24. The evidence of Maj. Gen. Nazar Hussain Shah (Witness No. 242 GOC 16 Div, Maj. Gen. M.H Ansari (Witness NO. 233) GOC, 9 Div, as well as of Brig. Baqir Siddiqui (Witness No. 218) Chief of Staff, Eastern Command, disclosed that these officers and their units were involved in large scale looting, including the theft of Rs. 1,35,00,000 from the National Bank Treasury at Siraj Ganj. This amount was intercepted by a JCO at the Paksi Bridge crossing when it was being carried in the lower part of the body of a truck. The driver of the truck produced a chit reading "released by Major Maddad." We were informed that a Court o Inquiry was conveyed under the Chairmanship of Maj. Gen. M.H Ansari who had recorded some evidence, but could not complete the inquiry owing to the outbreak of war.

25. The GHQ representative was not able to inform us as to what action had ultimately been taken by GIIQ in respect of these officers, except that Brig. Jehanzeb Arabab had been appointed to officiate as GOC of a Division. The Commission feels that this appointment, before the completion of the inquiry and exoneration of the officer from any blame, was highly inadvisable on the part of the GHQ. We recommend that action should now be taken without delay to finalise the proceedings of the inquiry commenced by Maj Gen Ansari in East Pakistan. There should be no difficulty in reconstructing the record, if necessary as the material witness appear to be now available in Pakistan.

26. Before we conclude this Chapter, we would like to state that we had no desire to embark on any inquiry into personal allegations of immorality an dishonestly against senior Army Commanders, but were persuaded to examine these matters owing to the universal belief that such in-

famous conduct had a direct hearing on the qualities of determination and leadership displayed by these officers in the 1971 war. We have regretfully found that this was indeed so. It is, therefore, imperative that deterrent action should be taken by the Government, wherever it is justified by the facts, in order to maintain the high moral standards and traditions for which the Muslim Army of Pakistan was justly proud before degeneration set in.

CHAPTER 2
ALLEGED ATROCITIES BY THE PAKISTAN ARMY

As is well-known, the conduct of the Pakistani army, while engaged in counter-insurgency measures is East Pakistan since March 1971, has come in for a lot of criticism from several quarters. We had occasion to deal with the subject in Paragraphs 5-8 of Chapter II of Part V of the main report. We have examined this question further in the light of fresh evidence recorded by us.

MISDEEDS OF THE AWAMI LEAGUE MILITANTS:

2. It is necessary that this painful chapter of the events in East Pakistan be looked at in its proper perspective. Let it not be forgotten that the initiative in resorting to violence and cruelty was taken by the militants of the Awami League, during the month of March, 1971, following General Yahya Khan's announcement of the 1st of March regarding the postponement of the session of the National Assembly scheduled for the 3rd of March 1971. It will be recalled that from the 1st of March to the 3rd of March

1971, the Awami League had taken complete control of East Pakistan, paralysing the authority of the federal government. There is reliable evidence to show that during this period the miscreants indulged in large scale massacres and rape against pro-Pakistan elements, in the towns of Dacca, Narayanganj, Chittagong, Chandraghona, Rangamati, Khulna, Dinajpur, Ghafargaoa, Kushtia, Ishurdi, Noakhali, Sylhet, Maulvi Bazaar, Rangpur, Saidpur, Jessore, Barisal, Mymensingh, Rajshahi, Pabna, Sirajgonj, Comilla, Brahman Baria, Bogra, Naugaon, Santahar, and several other smaller places.

3. Harrowing tales of these atrocities were narrated by the large number of West Pakistanis and Biharis who were able to escape from these places and reach the safety of West Pakistan. For days on end, all through the troubled month of March 1971, swarms of terrorised non-Bengalis lay at the Army-controlled Dacca airport awaiting their turn to be taken to the safety of West Pakistan. Families of West Pakistani officers and other ranks serving with East Bengal units were subjected to inhuman treatment, and a large number of West Pakistani officers were butchered by the erstwhile Bengali colleagues.

4. These atrocities were completely blacked out at the time by the Government of Pakistan for fear of retaliation by the Bengalis living in West Pakistan. The Federal Government did issue a White Paper in this behalf in August 1971, but unfortunately it did not create much impact for the reason that it was highly belated, and adequate publicity was not given to it in the national and international press.

5. However, recently, a renowned journalist of high-standing, Mr. Qutubuddin Aziz, has taken pains to marshal the evidence in a publication called "Blood and Tears." The book contains the harrowing tales of inhuman crimes committed on the helpless Biharis, West Pakistanis and patriotic Bengalis living in East Pakistan during that pe-

riod. According to various estimates mentioned by Mr. Qutubuddin Aziz, between 100,000 and 500,000 persons were slaughtered during this period by the Awami League militants.

6. As far as we can judge, Mr Qutubuddin Aziz has made use of authentic personal accounts furnished by the repatriates whose families, have actually suffered at the hands of the Awami League militants. He has also extensively referred to the contemporary accounts of foreign correspondents then stationed in East Pakistan. The plight of the non-Bengali elements still living in Bangladesh and the insistence of that Government on their large-scale repatriation to Pakistan, are factors which appear to confirm the correctness of the allegations made against the Awami League in this behalf.

PROVOCATION OF THE ARMY

7. We mention these facts not in justification of the atrocities or other crimes alleged to have been committed by the Pakistani Army during its operations in East Pakistan, but only to put the record straight and to enable the allegations to be judged in their correct perspective. The crimes committed by the Awami League miscreants were bound to arouse anger and bitterness in the minds of the troops, especially when they were not confined to barracks during these weeks immediately preceding the military action, but were also subjected to the severest of humiliations. They had seen their comrades insulted, deprived of food and ration, and even killed without rhyme or reason. Tales of wholesale slaughter of families of West Pakistani officers and personnel of several units had also reached the soldiers who were after all only human, and reacted violently in the process of restoring the authority of the Central Government

THE NATURE OF ALLEGATIONS

8. According to the allegations generally made, the excesses committed by the Pakistani Army fall into the following categories:-

a) Excessive use of force and fire power in Dacca during the night of the 25th and 26th of March 1971 when the military operation was launched.

b) Senseless and wanton arson and killings in the countryside during the course of the "sweeping operations" following the military action.

c) Killing of intellectuals and professionals like doctors, engineers, etc., and burying them in mass graves not only during early phases of the military action but also during the critical days of the war in December 1971.

d) Killing of Bengali Officers and men of the units of the East Bengal Regiment, East Pakistan Rifles and the East Pakistan Police Force in the process of disarming them, or on pretence of quelling their rebellion.

e) Killing of East Pakistani civilian officers, businessmen and industrialists, or their mysterious disappearance from their homes by or at the instance of Army Officers performing Martial Law duties.

f) Raping of a large number of East Pakistani women by the officers and men of the Pakistan army as a deliberate act of revenge, retaliation and torture.

g) Deliberate killing of members of the Hindu minority.

SUBSTANCE OF EVIDENCE

9. In view of the seriousness of the allegations, their persistence and their international impact as well as their fundamental importance from the point of view of moral

and mental discipline of the Pakistan Army, we made it a point of questioning the repatriated officers at some length in this behalf. We feel that a brief reference to some typical statements made before us by responsible military and civil officers will be instructive, and helpful in reaching the necessary conclusions.

10) Lt. Gen. A.A.K. Niazi, apparently in an endeavor to put the blame on his predecessor, then Lt. Gen. Tikka Khan, stated that "military action was based on use of force primarily, and at many places indiscriminate use of force was resorted to which alienated the public against the Army. Damage done during those early days of the military action could never be repaired, and earned for the military leaders names such as "Changez Khan" and "Butcher of East Pakistan." While the military action was on, the then Martial Law Administration alienated the world press by unceremoniously hounding out foreign correspondents from East Pakistan, thus losing out in the propaganda war to the Indians completely. "He went on to add: "on the assumption of command I was very much concerned with the discipline of troops, and on 15th of April, 1971, that is within four days of my command, I addressed a letter to all formations located in the area and insisted that loot, rape, arson, killing of people at random must stop and a high standard of discipline should be maintained. I had come to know that looted material had been sent to West Pakistan which included cars, refrigerators and air conditioners etc." When asked about the alleged killing of East Pakistani officers and men during the process of disarming, the General replied that he had heard something of the kind but all these things had happened in the initial stages of the military action before his time. He denied the allegation that he ever ordered his subordinates to exterminate the Hindu minority. He denied that any intellectuals were killed during December, 1971. He admitted that there were a few cases of rape, but asserted that the

guilty persons were duly punished. He also stated that "these things do happen when troops are spread over. My orders were that there would not be less than a company. When a company is there, there is an officer with them to control them but if there is a small picket like section, then it is very difficult to control. In Dacca jail we had about 80 persons punished for excesses."

11. Another significant statement was made in this regard by Maj. Gen. Rao Barman Ali, Adviser to the Governor of East Pakistan namely: "Harrowing tales of rape, loot, arson, harassment, and of insulting and degrading behaviour were narrated in general terms.... I wrote out an instruction to act as a guide for decent behaviour and recommended action required to be taken to win over the hearts of the people. This instruction under General Tikka Khan's signature was sent to Eastern Command. I found that General Tikka's position was also deliberately undermined and his instructions ignored...excesses were explained away by false and concocted stories and figures."

12. About the use of excessive force on the night between the 25th and 26th March 1971, we have a statement from Brigadier Shah Abdul Qasim (witness No. 267) to the effect that "no pitched battle was fought on the 25th of March in Dacca. Excessive force was used on that night. Army personnel acted under the influence of revenge and anger during the military operation." It has also been alleged that mortars were used to blast two Residence Halls, thus causing excessive casualties. In defence, it has been stated that these Halls were at the relevant time not occupied by the students but by Awami League insurgents, and were also being used as dumps for arms and ammunition stored by the Awami League for its armed rebellion.

13. Still another significant statement came from Brigadier Mian Taskeenuddin (Witness No. 282): "Many junior

and other officers took the law into their own hands to deal with the so-called miscreants. There have been cases of interrogation of miscreants which were far more severe in character than normal and in some cases blatantly in front of the public. The discipline of the Pakistani army as was generally understood had broken down. In a command area (Dhoom Ghat) between September and October miscreants were killed by firing squads. On coming to know about it I stopped the same forthwith."

14. Maj. Gen. Nazar Hussain Shah, GOC 16 Division, conceded that "there were rumors that Bengalis were disposed of without trial." Similarly, Brigadier Abdul Qadir Khan (Witness No. 243) Commander 93 (A) Bde., and Chairman of the Inter-Services Screening Committee, Dacca, admitted that "a number of instance of picking up Bengalis did take place." Lt. Col. S. S. H. Bokhari, CO of 29 Cavalry, appearing as Witness no 244, stated that "In Rangpur two officers and 30 men were disposed of without trial. It may have happened in other stations as well." An admission was also made by Lt. Col. S. M. Naeem (Witness No 258) CO of 39 Baluch that "innocent people were killed by us during sweep operations and it created estrangement amongst the public."

15. Lt Col. Mansoorul Haq, GSO-I, Division, appearing as Witness No 260, has made detailed and specific allegations as follows:

"A Bengali, who was alleged to be a Mukti Bahini or Awami Leaguer, was being sent to Bangladesh-a code name for death without trial, without detailed investigations and without any written order by any authorised authority."

Indiscriminate killing and looting could only serve the cause of the enemies of Pakistan. In the harshness, we lost the support of the silent majority of the people of East Pakistan.... The Comilla Cantt. massacre (on 27th/28th of March, 1971) under the orders of CO 53 Field Regiment,

34

Lt. Gen. Yakub Malik, in which 17 Bengali Officers and 915 men were just slain by a flick of one Officer's fingers should suffice as an example.

There was a general feeling of hatred against Bengalis amongst the soldiers and officers including Generals. There were verbal instructions to eliminate Hindus.

In Salda Nadi area about 500 persons were killed.

When the army moved to clear the rural areas and small towns, it moved in a ruthless manner, destroying, burning and killing. The rebels while retreating carried out reprisals against non-Bengalis.

16. Several civilian officers have also deposed in a similar vein, and it would suffice to quote here the words of Mr. Mohammad Ashraf, Additional Deputy Commissioner, Dacca, to whose evidence we have also referred earlier in another context. He stated that "after the military action the Bengalis were made aliens in their own homeland. The life, property, and honour of even the most highly placed among them were not safe. People were picked up from their homes on suspicion and dispatched to Bangladesh, a term used to describe summary executions. .... The victims included Army and Police Officers, businessmen, civilian officers etc....There was no Rule of Law in East Pakistan. A man had no remedy if he was on the wanted list of the Army.... Army Officers who were doing intelligence were raw hands, ignorant of the local language and callous of Bengali sensibilities."

17. About the attitude of senior officers in this behalf, Brigadier Iqbalur Rehman Shariff (Witness no. 269), has alleged that during his visit to formations in East Pakistan General Gul Hassan used to ask the soldiers "how many Bengalis have you shot."

18. The statements appearing in the evidence of Lt. Col. Aziz Ahmed Khan (Witness no 276) who was Command-

ing Officer 8 Baluch and then CO 86 Mujahid Battalion are also directly relevant. "Brigadier Arbbab also told me to destroy all houses in Joydepur. To a great extent I executed this order. General Niazi visited my unit at Thakurgaon and Bogra. He asked us how many Hindus we had killed. In May, there was an order in writing to kill Hindus. This order was from Brigadier Abdullah Malik of 23 Brigade."

19. While the extracts of evidence given above reflect the general position in regard to the allegations we are considering, it appears to be necessary to deal specifically with certain matters brought to the notice of the Prime Minister of Pakistan by the Bangladesh authorities, or which have otherwise been particularly mentioned by certain witnesses appearing before the Commission during the present session.

Painting the Green of East Pakistan Red

20. During his meeting with the Prime Minister of Pakistan at Dacca on Friday, the 28th of June 1974, the Bangladesh Prime Minister Sk. Mujibur Rahman, complained inter-alia that Maj Gen Rao Farman Ali had written in his own hand on Government stationery that "The green of East Pakistan will have to be painted red." Sk. Mujibur Rahman promised to supply a photostat copy of this document to the Government of Pakistan." The same has since been received and is added to Annexure "A" to this chapter. The insinuation is that this writing amounted to a written declaration of the intentions of the Pakistan Army and the martial law administration in East Pakistan to indulge in large-scale bloodshed in order to suppress the movement for Bangladesh. This writing is being put forward as a proof of the killings alleged to have been carried out in East Pakistan during the military operations.

21. We asked Maj. Gen. Farman Ali to explain the significance of this writing and the circumstances under which it came to me made by him. He has stated that the words "the green of East Pakistan will have to be painted red" were uttered by one of the NPA leaders in Paltan Maidan, Dacca in a public speech during June 1970. The Martial Law headquarters thought that these words had been uttered by Mr Mohammad Toha of the NAP, and the General was asked to call for the explanation of Mr Toha and warn him not to say things prejudicial to public peace. To remind himself he wrote these words down on the back of his table diary, when they were repeated to him on telephone by Lt. Gen. Yakub, the then Zonal Martial Law administrator in East Pakistan. Toha later denied having uttered these words and mentioned the names of Qazi Zafar and Rashid Menon in this connection. As these gentlemen had gone underground, General Farman Ali could not take any further action against them. The General has further explained that as Mr Toha and his associates had communist leanings, these words were intended to convey their conviction and objective that East Pakistan would be turned into a communist state, and not that there would be bloodshed. Finally, Maj. Gen. Farman Ali has stated that he did not give any importance to this note and it must have fallen into the hands of his Bengali Personal Assistant, when the diary for the year 1970 was replaced at the close of that year.

22. From the photostat copy sent to the Government of Pakistan by the Government of Bangladesh, it becomes clear that the paper on which these words are written was apparently in the nature of a writing pad on which notes are jotted down as an aid to memory. The paper bears the heading:-

"Governor's Secretariat, East Pakistan"

Then there are miscellaneous entries, which do not have any connection with each other, for instance,

"Siraj - Iqbal Hall, D.U."

Below these words a line in ink is drawn and then appear the words "Case against Mr. Toha and others." These words are followed by the telephone number of the Chief Justice and then by some other entries relating to some accommodation and the name of one Mr. Karamat. Then appear the words in question, enclosed by a circle in black ink. There is a further entry of an Officer's name below these words, which apparently has no connection with this matter.

23. A perusal of this document leave no doubt in our mind that it was indeed in the nature of a writing pad or table diary on which the General made miscellaneous notes during course of his work. The words "Case against Mr Toha and others," appearing in the same page, do support Maj. Gen. Farman Ali's contention that it was in this connection that he noted these words to remind himself, while confronting Mr Toha as directed by the Martial Law Administrator. We consider that it is highly fanciful to regard this note as being in the nature of a solemn declaration of Maj. Gen. Farman Ali's intention to shed blood on the soil of East Pakistan. The explanation given by the General appears to us to be correct.

Alleged Killing of Intellectuals during December 1971

24. This again is a matter, which was specifically raised by Sk. Mujibur Rehman during his meeting with the Prime Minister at Dacca. According to Maj. Gen. Farman Ali it was on the 9th and 10th of December 1971 that he was rung up in the evening by Maj. Gen. Jamshed, who was the Deputy Martial Law Administrator for Dacca Division and asked to come to his headquarters in Peelkhana. On

reaching the headquarters he saw a large number of vehicles parked there. Maj. Gen. Jamshed was getting into a car and he asked Maj. Gen. Farman Ali to come along. They both drove to Headquarters of Eastern Command to meet Lt. Gen. Niazi and on the way Maj. Gen. Jamshed informed Maj. Gen. Farman that they were thinking of arresting certain people. Gen. Farman Ali advised against it. On reaching Lt. General Niazi's headquarters he repeated his advice, on which Lt. Gen. Niazi kept quiet and so did Maj. Gen. Jamshed. Maj. Gen. Farman Ali has stated that he cannot say anything as to what happened after he came away from the headquarters but he thinks that no further action was taken.

25. When questioned on this point, Lt. Gen. A. A. K. Niazi stated that the local Commanders had, on the 9th of December 1971, brought a list to him which included the names of miscreants, heads of Mukti Bahini etc., but not any intellectuals but he had stopped them from collecting and arresting these people. He denied the allegation that any intellectuals were in fact arrested and killed on the 9th December 1971 or thereafter.

26. Maj. Gen. Jamshed has, however, a slightly different version to offer. He says that it was on the 9th and 10th of December 1971 that General Niazi expressed his apprehension of a general uprising in the Dacca city and ordered him to examine the possibility of arresting certain persons according to lists which were already with the various agencies, namely the Martial Law Authorities and the Intelligence Branch. A conference was held on the 9th and 10th of December 1971 in which these lists were produced by the agencies concerned and the total number of persons to be arrested came to about two or three thousand. According to him, arrangements for accommodation, security guards, missing and the safety of the arrested persons from bombing/strafing by the Indian Air Force presented insurmountable problems and therefore,

he reported back to Lt. Gen. Niazi that the proposal be dropped. He states that thereafter no further action was taken in this matter.

27. From the statements made by the three Generals who appear to be directly concerned in the matter, it seems that although there was some talks of arresting persons known to be leaders of the Awami League or Mukti Bahini so as to prevent chances o a general uprising in Dacca during the closing phases of the war with India, yet no practical action was taken in view of the circumstances then prevailing, namely the precarious position of the Pakistan Army and the impending surrender. We consider, therefore, that unless the Bangladesh authorities can produce some convincing evidence, it is not possible to record a finding that any intellectuals or professionals were indeed arrested and killed by the Pakistan Army during December 1971.

Killings During Disarming of East Pakistan Units

28. In the evidence specific allegations were made before the Commission that Lt. Col. Yakub Malik, CO of 53 Field Regiment was responsible for the killing of 17 Officers and 915 other ranks at Comilla Cantt., while disarming 4 EBR, 40 Field Ambulance and Bengali SSG personnel. An explanation was accordingly called from this officer, in which he has denied the allegation, and has asserted that resistance was put up by the particular units aforementioned as a result of which casualties were sustained on both sides. He asserts, however, that in April 1971 when the situation stabilised a large number of disarmed Bengali personnel detained in the barracks were reported to Headquarters 9 Div., thus implying that no such killing took place during the disarming process towards the end of March 1971.

29. Similar allegations have also been made before the Commission regarding the disarming of East Pakistani personnel of 29 Cavalry at Rangpur, although the number of persons said to have been killed is mentioned as being only two officers and 30 other ranks. An explanation was called from the Commanding Officer, Brigadier, Saghir Hussain and he has denied the allegation stating that all the personnel, barring a few who had either deserted or did not return from leave, were safely evacuated to West Pakistan under arrangements of Eastern Command, and they were later repatriated to Bangladesh along with other East Pakistani personnel.

30. The evidence before the Commission in respect of these allegations is obviously not conclusive. It is possible that there may have been other instances of casualties inflicted during the disarming of East Pakistani personnel. The Commission feels that the Army authorities must conduct a thorough inquiry into these matters so as to elicit the truth and fix responsibility.

MAGNITUDE OF ATROCITIES

31. In the circumstances that prevailed in East Pakistan from the 1st of March to the 16th of December 1971, it was hardly possible to obtain an accurate estimate of the toll of death and destruction caused by the Awami League militants and later by the Pakistan Army. It must also be remembered that even after the military action of the 25th of march 1971, Indian infiltrators and members of the Mukti Bahini sponsored by the Awami League continued to indulge in killings, rape and arson during their raids on peaceful villages in East Pakistan, not only in order to cause panic and disruption and carry out their plans of subversion, but also to punish those East Pakistanis who were not willing to go along with them. In any estimate of the extent of atrocities alleged to have been committed

on the East Pakistani people, the death and destruction caused by the Awami League militants throughout this period and the atrocities committed by them on their own brothers and sisters must, therefore, be always be kept in view.

32. According to the Bangladesh authorities, the Pakistan Army was responsible for killing three million Bengalis and raping 200,000 East Pakistani women. It does not need any elaborate argument to see that these figures are obviously highly exaggerated. So much damage could not have been caused by the entire strength of the Pakistan Army then stationed in East Pakistan even if it had nothing else to do. In fact, however, the army was constantly engaged in fighting the Mukti Bahini, the Indian infiltrators, and later the Indian army. It has also the task of running the civil administration, maintaining communications and feeding 70 million people of East Pakistan. It is, therefore, clear that the figures mentioned by the Dacca authorities are altogether fantastic and fanciful.

33. Different figures were mentioned by different persons in authority but the latest statement supplied to us by the GHQ shows approximately 26,000 persons killed during the action by the Pakistan Army. This figure is based on situation reports submitted from time to time by the Eastern Command to the General Headquarters. It is possible that even these figures may contain an element of exaggeration as the lower formations may have magnified their own achievements in quelling the rebellion. However, in the absence of any other reliable date, the Commission is of the view that the latest figure supplied by the GHQ should be accepted. An important consideration which has influenced us in accepting this figure as reasonably correct is the fact that the reports were sent from East Pakistan to GHQ at a time when the Army Officers in East Pakistan could have had no notion whatsoever of any accountability in this behalf.

34. The falsity of Sheikh Mujibur Rahman's repeated allegation that Pakistani troops had raped 200,000 Bengali girls in 1971 was borne out when the abortion team he had commissioned from Britain in early 1972 found that its workload involved the termination of only a hundred or more pregnancies.

QUESTION OF RESPONSIBILITY

35. For almost three years now, the world has repeatedly heard a list of 195 names said to have been prepared by the Dacca authorities in connection with the commission of these atrocities and crimes. As the Commission has not been supplied with a copy of this list, it is not possible for us to comment upon the justification or otherwise of the inclusion of any particular names therein. It is, however, clear that the final and overall responsibility must rest on General Yahya Khan, Lt. Gen. Pirazada, Maj Gen. Umar, Lt. Gen. Mitha. It has been brought out in evidence that Maj. Gen. Mitha was particularly active in East Pakistan in the days preceding the military action of the 25th of March 1971, and even the other Generals just mentioned were present in Dacca along with Yahya Khan, and secretly departed there on the evening of that fateful day after fixing the deadline for the military action. Maj. Gen. Mitha is said to have remained behind. There is also evidence that Lt. Gen Tikka Khan, Major Gen. Farman Ali and Maj. Gen Khadim Hussain were associated with the planning of the military action. There is, however, nothing to show that they contemplated the use of excessive force or the Commission of atrocities and excesses on the people of East Pakistan.

36. The immediate responsibility for executing the plan of this action fell on Lt. Gen. Tikka Khan who succeeded Lt. Gen. Mohammad Yakub on the 7th of March 1971 as Zonal Administrator, Martial Law, as well as Commander East-

ern Command. This last responsibility was passed on by him to Lt. Gen. A.A.K. Niazi on the 7th of April 1971. From that day until the day of surrender the troops in East Pakistan remained under the operational control of Lt. Gen. Niazi who also assumed powers of the Martial Law administrator on the appointment of a civilian Governor in August 1971. It is a question for determination as to what share of responsibility must rest on these commanders for the excesses allegedly committed by the troops under their Command. It is in evidence that Lt. Gen. Tikka Khan was always willing to redress grievances and take disciplinary action whenever complaints of excesses were brought to his notice. It has also to be said that both these Generals had issued repeated warnings to troops to refrain from acts of violence and immorality. At the same time there is some evidence to suggest that the words and personal actions of Lt. Gen. Niazi were calculated to encourage the killings and rape.

37. The direct responsibility of the alleged excesses and atrocities must, of course, rest on those officers and men who physically perpetuated them or knowingly and deliberately allowed them to be so perpetuated. These officers and men not only showed lack of discipline in disobeying the directives of the Eastern Command and Zonal Martial Law Administrator, but also indulged in criminal acts punishable under the Army Act as well as the ordinary law of the land.

CONCLUSIONS AND RECOMMENDATIONS

38. From what we have said in the preceding Paragraphs it is clear that there is substance in the allegations that during and after the military action excesses were indeed committed on the people of East Pakistan, but the versions and estimates put forward by the Dacca authorities are highly coloured and exaggerated. Some of the incidents

alleged by those authorities did not take place at all, and on others fanciful interpretations have been deliberately placed for the purpose of maligning the Pakistan army and gaining world sympathy. We have also found that the strong provocation was offered to the army owing to the misdeeds of the Awami League. It has also been stated that use of force was undoubtedly inherent in the military action required to restore the authority of the Federal Government. Nevertheless, in spite of all these factors we are of the view that the officers charged with the task of restoring law and order were under an obligation to act with restraint and to employ only the minimum force necessary for the purpose. No amount of provocation by the militants of the Awami League or other miscreants could justify retaliation by a disciplined army against its own people. The Pakistan Army was called upon to operate in Pakistan territory, and could not, therefore, be permitted to behave as if it was dealing with external aggression or operating on enemy soil. Irrespective, therefore, of the magnitude of the atrocities, we are of the considered opinion that it's necessary for the Government of Pakistan to take effective action to punish those who were responsible for the commission of these alleged excesses and atrocities.

INQUIRIES AND TRIALS

39. On the basis of the evidence coming before the Commission, we have been able to indicate only in general terms the direct and indirect responsibility of certain senior commanders and others, but the question of fixing individual responsibility and awarding punishment appropriate thereto need to be determined according to the prescribed procedures available under the Pakistan Army Act and other applicable laws of the land. We would, accordingly, reiterate the recommendation made by us in Paragraph 7 of Chapter III of Para V of the main report that

the Government of Pakistan should set up a high-powered Court or Commission of Inquiry to investigate these allegations, and to hold trials of those who indulged in these atrocities, brought a bad name to the Pakistan Army and alienated the sympathies of the local population by their acts of wanton cruelty and immorality against our own people. The composition of the Court of Inquiry, if not its proceedings, should be publicly announced so as to satisfy national conscience and international opinion.

40. The Commission feels that sufficient evidence is now available in Pakistan for a fruitful inquiry to be undertaken in this regard. As the Government of Bangladesh has been recognised by Pakistan, it may be feasible to request the Dacca authorities to forward to this Court of Inquiry whatever evidence may be available with them.

CHAPTER 3

PROFESSIONAL RESPONSIBILITIES OF CERTAIN SENIOR ARMY COMMANDERS

In Chapters 1, 2 and 5 of Part 5 of the main report we have dealt with the moral and disciplinary aspects of the events and causes leading to the defeat of the Pakistan Army in the 1971 war, and have also touched upon the individual responsibility of certain senior officers. In the preceding two chapters of the Supplementary Report, we have offered further observations on these aspects and have commented upon the conduct of certain Army Officers posted in East Pakistan. There, however, still remains the question of determining whether any disciplinary action is called for against certain senior army commanders for

47

their failings in the discharge of their professional duties in the conduct ad prosecution of the war in East Pakistan.

NATURE OF DISCIPLINARY ACTION

2. In view of the glaring weaknesses and negligence displayed by some of the senior officers operating in East Pakistan, we have anxiously considered the nature of the disciplinary action required in the case. We find that there are several provisions in the Pakistan Army Act 1952 having a direct bearing on this matter. In the first place, there is section 24 which is in the following terms:- "24. Offences in relation to enemy and punishable with death. Any person to this Act who commits any of the following offenses, that is to say,-

(a) Shamefully abandons or delivers up any garrison, fortress, airfield, place, post or guard committed to his charge or which it is his duty to defend, or uses any means to compel or induce any commanding officer or any other person to do any of the said acts; or

(b) in the presence of any enemy, shamefully casts away his arms, ammunition, tools or equipment, or misbehaves in such manner as to show cowardice; or

(c) intentionally uses word or any other means to compel or induce any person subject to this Act, or to the Indian Air Force Act, 1932 (XIV of 1932) or Pakistan Air Force Act 1953 or to the Pakistan Navy Ordinance, 1961, to abstain from acting against the enemy or to discourage such persons from acting against the enemy; or

(d) directly or indirectly, treacherously holds correspondence with or communicates intelligence to, the enemy or who coming to the knowledge of such correspondence or communication treacherously omits to discover it to his commanding or other superior officer; or

48

(e) directly or indirectly assists or relies the enemy with arm, ammunition, equipment, supplies or money or knowingly harbours or protects an enemy not being a prisoner; or

(f) treacherously or through cowardice sends a flag of truce to the enemy; or

(g) in time of war, of during any operation, intentionally occasions a false alarm in action, camp, garrison or quarters, or spreads reports calculated to create alarm or despondency; or

(h) in time of action, leaves his commanding officer, or quits his post, guard, piquet, patrol or party without being regularly relieved or without leave; or

(i) having being made a prisoner of war, voluntarily serves with or aids the enemy; or \

(j) knowingly does when on active service any act calculated to imperil success of the Pakistan forces or any forces-operating therewith or of any part of such forces' shall, on conviction by court martial, be punished with death or with such less punishment as it is in this Act mentioned."

3. Section 25 is also relevant, and reads as under:-

25. Offences in relation to the enemy and not punishable with death. Any person subject to this Act who, on active service -

(a) without order from his superior officer leaves the ranks in order to secure prisoner, animals or materials, or on the pretence of taking wounded men to the rear; or

(b) without orders from his superior officer, willfully destroys or damages any property; or

(c) is taken prisoner for want of due precaution or through disobedience of orders or wilful neglect of duty, or, having been taken prisoner, fails to rejoin service when he is able to do so; or

(d) without due authority, either holds correspondence with, or communicates intelligence, or sends a flag of truce to the enemy; or

(e) by words of mouth, or in writing, or by signals, or otherwise spreads reports calculated to create alarm or despondency; or

(f) in action, or previously to going into action, uses words calculated to create alarm or despondency; shall on conviction by court martial, be punished with rigorous imprisonment for a term which may extend to fourteen years, or with much less punishment as is in this Act mentioned."

4. Finally, there is section 55 which is of a general nature, and provides;- "55. Violation of good order and discipline- Any person subject to this Act who is guilty of any act, conduct, disorder and of military discipline shall , on conviction by court martial, be punished with rigorous imprisonment for a term which may extend to five years, or with such less punishment as is in this Act mentioned."

5. We are fully cognizant of the fact that defeat in war, even entailing surrender, is not necessarily punishable as a military offence unless it has been occasioned by wilful neglect of the Commander concerned in the performance of his duties in respect of the appreciation of the situation regarding the enemy's intention, strength, own resources, terrain, etc; or in the planning and conduct of the operations; or a wilful failure to take action as required under the circumstances. A callous disregard of the recognised techniques and principles of warfare would clearly amount to culpable negligence, and could not be excused as an honest error of judgement. A deliberate failure to

adopt the proper course of action to meet a certain contingency cannot be covered by taking shelter behind the plea that his superiors did not advise him properly in time. It further appears to us that every Commander must be presumed to possess the calibre and quality, appurtenant to his rank, and he must per force bear full responsibility for all the acts of omission and commission, leading to his defeat in war, which are clearly attributable to culpable negligence on his part to take the right action at the right time, as distinguished from (illegible) or circumstances beyond his control. He would also be liable to be punished if he shows a lack of will to fight and surrenders to the enemy at a juncture when he still had the resources and the capability to put up resistance. Such an act would appear to fall clearly under clause (a) of section 24 of the Pakistan Army Act.

NEED AND JUSTIFICATION FOR TRIAL AND PUNISHMENT

6. Having heard the views of a large number of witnesses drawn from all sections of society, professions and services, the Commission feels that there is consensus on the imperative need to book these senior army commanders who have brought disgrace and defeat to Pakistan by their professional incompetence, culpable negligence and wilful neglect in the performance of their duties, and physical and moral cowardice in abandoning the fight when they had the capability and resources to resist the enemy. We are also of the view that proper and firm disciplinary action , and not merely retirement from service, is necessary to ensure against any future recurrence of the kind of shameful conduct displayed during the 1971 war. We believe that such action would not only satisfy the nations demand for punishment where it is deserved, but would also serve to emphasise the concept of professional accountability which appears to have been forgotten by se-

nior army officers since their involvement in politics, civil administration and Martial Law duties.

CASES REQUIRING ACTION BY WAY OF COURT MARTIAL

7. In Part III of the present report, we have discussed and analysed at some length the concept of defence of East Pakistan adopted by Lt. Gen Niazi, and the manner in which he and his Divisional and Brigade Commanders formulated their plans to implement that concept within the resources available to them in East Pakistan. We have then narrated the important events involving the surrender of well-defended strong points and fortresses without a fight, desertion of his area of responsibility by a Divisional Commander, disintegration of brigades and battalions in frantic and foolish efforts to withdraw from certain posts , and abandoning of the wounded and the sick is a callous disregard of all human and military values. We have also seen how the Eastern Command had failed to plan for an all out war with India and particularly to provide for the defence of Dacca which had been described as the political and military lynch-pin of East Pakistan. We have also described the painful events leading to the ultimate surrender of such a large body of men and materials to the Indian Army at juncture when, by all accounts, the Pakistan Army was still able to put up resistance for anything up to two weeks or more. In this context we have also taken note of the inexplicable orders issued by the Eastern Command to stop the destruction of war before material before the surrender , and the abject and shameful attitude adopted by the Commander, Eastern Command, at various stages of the surrender ceremonies in the presence of the Indian Generals. Finally, we have observed that during his period of captivity at Jabbalpur (India) Lt General Niazi made efforts to persuade, by threats and inducements, his subordinate Commanders to present a coordinated story so as to mitigate his responsibility for the debate.

8. Judged in the light of this analysis of the events leading to the surrender of our surrender of our Army in East Pakistan, and the relevant provisions of the Pakistan Army Act and the considerations thereto, as outlined in the preceding Paragraphs, we are of the considered opinion that the following senior officers ought to be tried by court martial on the charges listed against them , and we recommend accordingly.

(1) Lt. Gen. A.A.K. Niazi, Commander, Eastern Command

(i) That he willfully failed to appreciate the imminence of all-out war with India, in spite of all indications to the contrary, namely the declarations of the Indian Prime Minister and other important Government leaders, the signing of the Indo-Soviet treaty in August, 1971, the amassing of eight divisions of the Indian Army, eleven squadrons of the Indian Air Force, and a large task force of the Indian Navy in and around East Pakistan , and the clear warning given to him by the GHQ on the basis of reliable intelligence regarding Indian plans of invasion of East Pakistan, with the n consequence that he continued to deploy his troops in a forward posture although that deployment had become entirely unsuited for defence against open Indian aggression;

(ii) That he displayed utter lack of professional competence, initiative and foresight, expected of an Army Commander of his ran, seniority and experience, in not realising that the parts of his mission concerning anti-insurgency operations and ensuring that "no chunk of territory" was to be allowed to be taken over by the rebels for establishing Bangladesh, had become irrelevant in the context of the imminence of all-out attack by India on or about the 21st of November ,1971, and that the mast important part of his mission from that juncture onwards was to "defend

East Pakistan against external aggression"' and "keep the Corps in being and ensure the entity of East Pakistan"' with the result that he failed to concentrate his forces in time , which failure later led to fatal results;

(iii) That he displayed culpable negligence in adopting the concept of fortresses and strong points without fully understanding its technical implications as regards their ability to lend mutual support, availability of the necessary reserves to strike at the enemy in the event of his by passing any of the fortresses or overwhelming them with superior numbers , and the existence of a non-hostile population, with the disastrous consequence that was forced to surrender even though several of the fortresses and strong points were still intact on the 16th of December, 1971;

(iv) That he was guilty of criminal negligence in not including in his operational instruction No. 4 of 1971, issued on the 15th of July, 1971, any clear directive for a planned withdrawal of forces behind natural river obstacles to face the Indian onslaught and to defend what may be described as the Dacca Triangle for the purpose of keeping East Pakistan in being by giving up non-vital territory;

(v) That he in fact showed wilful neglect and culpable negligence of the worst order in failing to make any positive plan for the defence of Dacca;

(vi) That he displayed lack of generalship and mature judgement in requiring his subordinate commanders to simultaneously maintain a forward defence posture, occupy unmanned fortresses, and yet not withdraw from any position without sustaining 75% casualties and obtaining clearance from two-up, a variation from the norm of one-up, with the result that several formation commanders felt confused and bewildered and acted in a manner prejudicial to the sound conduct of operations and resulting in unnecessary casualties, as well as disorder and chaos arising from haphazard and unplanned withdrawals under pressure from the enemy;

(vii) That he displayed culpable negligence and wilful disregard of established principles of warfare by denuding Dacca of all regular troops by moving out 53 Brigade, which had been previously held as Corps reserve, on the expectation that he would be getting more troops as agreed to by GHQ on the 19th of November, 1971;

(viii) That he was guilty of criminal negligence in not ensuring beforehand satisfactory arrangements for transport, ferries, etc., with the result that even his last minute desperate efforts to withdraw troops from forward positions for the defence of Dacca were unsuccessful, and whatever troops did manage to reach Dacca did so minus their heavy equipment, besides suffering unnecessary casualties en route.

(ix) That he willfully failed to defend Dacca, and agreed to a shameful and premature surrender in spite of his own assertion before the Commission that Indians would have required at least a period of seven days to mount the offensive and another week to reduce the defences of Dacca, notwithstanding the shortcomings of his concept and plans, inadequacies and handicaps in respect of men and materials as compared to the enemy, the absence of air support and the presence of Mukti Bahini in and around Dacca.

(x) That he deliberately and willfully sent unduly pessimistic and alarming reports to GHQ with a view to eliciting permission to surrender as he had lost the will to fight as early as the 6th or 7th of December, 1971, owing to his own mismanagement of the entire of war and his inability to influence , inspire and guide the subordinate Commanders;

(xi) That he willfully, and for motives and reasons difficult to understand and appreciate, stopped the implementation of denial plans, with the result that large quantities of valuable war materials wee handed over intact to the Indian forces after surrender, in spite of the fact that GHQ had specifically ordered by their Signal of the 10th December ,1971, to carry out denial plans;

(xii) That he displayed a shameful and abject attitude in agreeing too surrender when he had himself offered a cease-fire to the Indian Commander-in-Chief; in signing the surrender document agreeing to lay down arms to the joint command of the Indian forces and the Mukti Bahini; in being present at the Dacca Airport to receive the victorious Indian General Arora; in ordering his own ADC to present a guard of honour to the said General; and in accepting the Indian proposal for a public surrender ceremony which brought everlasting shame to the Pakistan Army.

(xiii) That he was guilty of conduct unbecoming a Officer and Commander of his rank and seniority in that he acquired a notorious reputation for sexual immorality and indulgence in the smuggling of Pan from East to West Pakistan, with the inevitable consequence that he failed to inspire respect and confidence in the mind of his subordinates impaired his qualities of leadership and determination, and also encouraged laxity in discipline and moral standards among the officers and men under his command;

(xiv) That during the period of his captivity as a prisoner of war in Jabbalpur (India) and on repatriation to the Pakistan he made efforts to subvert the truth by trying to exercise undue influence on his Divisional and Brigade Commanders by offering them threats and inducements , so as to persuade them to present before the GHQ Briefing Committee and the Commission of Inquiry , a coordinated and coloured version of the events in East Pakistan for the purpose of mitigating his own responsibility for the defeat; and

(xv) That, on repatriation to Pakistan, he deliberately adopted a false and dishonest stand to the effect that he was willing and able to fight but was ordered to surrender by General Yahya Khan, and that as a dutiful soldier he had no option but to obey the said order against his best judgement.

2. MAJ GEN MOHAMMAD JAMSHED, EX-JOC 36 (AD HOC) DIVISION, DACCA

(i) That having been appointed as GOC 36 (ad hoc) Division for the express purpose of taking over from 14 Div., major responsibility for the defence of Dacca, he willfully failed to plan for the same, in accordance with sound principles of warfare, and showed culpable lack of initiative in this behalf;

(ii) That in the aforesaid capacity he willfully neglected to point out to Lt Gen Niazi, during various conference, the inadequacy of the resources at his disposal for the defence of Dacca, pointing out after the 19th of Nov, 1971, when 53 Brigade was sent out of Dacca to Feni;

(iii) That he displayed gross neglect in ordering the abrupt withdrawal of 93 Brigade from Jamalpur to Dacca without planning for it, well knowing that it was defending Dacca by holding that fortress, and in consequence of this ill-planed move 93 Brigade got completely disintegrated en route owing to the capture by the enemy of the Brigade Commander and a considerable portion of the Brigade;

(iv) That he showed complete lack of courage and will to fight in that he acquiesced in the decision of the Commander, Eastern Command, to surrender to surrender to the Indian forces at a juncture when it was still possible, in spite of the paucity of resources, to hold the enemy for a period of two weeks or so;

(v) That he deliberately and willfully neglected to inform the authorities concerned, on his repatriation to Pakistan, about the facts that he had got distributed Rs 50,000 out of Pakistan currency notes and other funds at his disposal or under his control, amongst certain evacuated from Dacca on the morning of December, 1971, and the manner in which he did so.

(3) Maj Gen M. Rahim Khan, ex-GOC 39 (ad hoc) Division

(a) In Paragraphs 9 to 11 of Chapter III of P art V of the Main Report , we had occasion to comment upon the conduct of Maj. Gen. Rahim Khan, GOC 39 (ad hoc) Division, who abandoned his Division , and evacuated his Divisional HQ from Chandpur , of course, with the permission of the Commander, Eastern Commander, with no replacement, and with the consequence that his Division disintegrated and had to be replaced with another Headquarter called the Narayan Sector Headquarters under a Brigadier. We had then recounted that the conduct of Maj Gen Rahim Khan in abandoning his troops and shifting to a place outside his area of responsibility prima facie called for a proper inquiry to determine whether the General was guilty of dereliction of duty or/and cowardice. We also added some other points which needed to be looked into in this behalf.

(b) As Maj Gen Rahim Khan was one of the senior officers serving in East Pakistan during the war, he voluntarily appeared before the Commission during the present session, primarily for the purpose of clearing his position. As will be seen from a detailed discussion of the operation of the 39 (ad hoc) Division in the narration of the military events, the Commission is far from satisfied with the performance of this General Officer. In the light of the information now available we now consider that he should be tried by a court martial on the following charges:

(i) That he shameful cowardice and undue regard for his personal safety in seeking, and obtaining, permission from the Eastern Command to abandon his Division and vacate his Divisional Headquarters from Chandpur on the 8th of December 1971, simply because Chandpur was threatened by the enemy, with the result that he deserted his troops and his area of responsibility in the middle of the war with India;

(ii) That y his wilful insistence on moving by day against competent advise, owing to fear of Mukti Bahini, caused the death of fourteen Naval ratings and four officers of his own HQ, besides injuries to several others, and to himself due to strafing by Indian aircraft;

(iii) That in his anxiety to get away from Chandpur, he willfully abandoned valuable signal equipment with the result that the communication system of the Division disintegrated and his subordinate commanders and troops were left to their own fate;

(iv) That he on the 12th of December, 1971, by word of mouth, caused alarm and despondency by General Niazi, Jamshed and Farman Ali that "it is all over , let us call it a day'" and that the Mukti Bahini might resort to massacre'

(v) That he willfully avoided submitting a debriefing report to GHQ, on being specially evacuated to Pakistan in early 1971, so as to conceal the circumstances of his desertion from his Div HQ at Chandpur with the consequence that the authorities were persuaded to appoint hi as Chief of the General Staff without any knowledge of his performance in East Pakistan.

4. BRIG. G.M. BAQIR SIDDIQUI, FORMER COS, EASTERN COMMAND, DACCA

(i) That as Chief of Staff, Eastern Command, he was guilty of wilful neglect in failing to advise the Commander , Eastern Commander, on sound professional lines in regard to the matters mentioned in charges (i) to (ix) framed against Lt. Gen Niazi;

(ii) That he willfully collaborated with, and assisted, the Commander, Eastern Command, in sending unduly pessimistic and alarming reports and signals to GHQ with a view to elicit permission to surrender, as he had also lost the will to fight owing to his culpable negligence and failure in the performance of his professional duties as the Chief of Staff of the Eastern Command;

(iii) That he showed culpable disregard of sound principles of planning for the war in that he excluded the Commanders of the supporting arms like signals, engineers, logistics, medical, etc. from full participation before the plans of the Eastern Command were finalized, with the result that the full benefit of the advice of these Commanders was not available to Lt. Gen. Niazi at the proper time;

(iv) That he was guilty of culpable negligence in not properly advising the Commander, Eastern Command, of the imminence and enormity of the Indian threat even though he had been fully briefed in this behalf by the GHQ at a conference in Rawalpindi in October 1971, and he also similarly failed to advise the Commander on the imperative need of readjusting troops to meet this threat;

(v) That he was responsible for abrupt changes in command in the middle of the war , and also for giving orders to subordinate formations over the head of their superior commanders, thus resulting in uncertainty and confusion during the critical days of the war;

(vi) That he willfully, and for motives and reasons difficult to understand and appreciate stopped the implementation of denial plans with the result that large quantities of valuable war materials were handed over intact to the Indian forces after the surrender, in spite of the fact the GHQ had specifically ordered by their of the 10th December 1971 to carry out denial plans;

(vii) That in particular, he instructed the commander Signals to keep the inter-wing transmitter in operation even after the surrender, apparently for the purpose of conveying recommendations to GHQ for the grant of gallantry awards etc. with the result that this valuable equipment fell intact into the hands of the enemy;

(viii) That he was unduly friendly with the enemy during the period of his captivity, so much so that he was allowed to go out shopping in Calcutta, a facility not allowed to anyone else by the Indians;

(ix) That he acted against good order and the custom of the Service in being instrumental in conveying threats and inducements to formation commanders for the purpose of presenting a coordinated story before the GHQ and the Commission of Inquiry in regard to the events leading to surrender in East Pakistan.

5. Brig Mohammad Hayat, former Comd. 107 bde. (9 Div)

(i) That as Commander 107 Bde., he displayed neglect in not formulating a sound plan for the defence of the fortress of Jessore;

(ii) That while launching counter attack at Gharibpur he neglected to obtain full information about the enemy strength, and did not himself command this important Brigade counter attack, in consequence whereof he lost seven tanks, his men suffered heavy casualties, and the defence of Jessore fortress was seriously jeopardised;

(iii) That on a report that enemy tanks had broken through the defences of Jessore he, without even verifying the same, shamefully abandoned the fortress of Jessore without a fight on the 6th of December 1971, delivering intact to the enemy all supplies and ammunition dumps stocked in the fortress, and without issuing any orders to his unit in contact with the enemy, who had to fight their own way during the following night.

(iv) That after abandoning Jessore without contact with the enemy, he withdrew to Khulna in wilful and intentional violation of the clear orders of G.Q.C. 9 Division to withdraw to Magura in the event of a forced withdrawal fro Jessore, thus making it impossible for the Divisional Commander to give battle to the enemy across the Madhumati River.

6. Brig. Mohammad Asla Niazi, former Cod., 53 Bde (39 Ad hoc Div.)

(i) That as Commander 53 Bde. he displayed culpable lack of initiative, determination and planning ability in that he failed to prepared defences of Mudafarganj as ordered by the G.O.C. 39 (Ad hoc) Division on the 4th of December 1971, with the result that the place was occupied by the enemy on or about the 6th of December 1971 , thus seriously endangering the line of communication between Tripura and Chandpur where the Divisional Headquarters was located;

(ii) That he showed culpable lack of courage, planning ability and determination in failing to eject the enemy fro Mudafarganj as ordered by the GOC on the 6th of December 1971, with the result that contingents of 23 Punjab and elements of 21 A.K. surrendered to an Indian unit on the

11th of December 1971 in highly adverse circumstances, without water or food and the ammunition having been nearly exhausted;

(iii) That he shamefully abandoned the Fortress of Laksham on or about the 9th of December 1971, which it was his duty to defend;

(iv) That he displayed wilful neglect in failing to properly organize ex-filtration of his troops fro the fortress at Laksham to Comilla on the 9th of December 1971, with the result that out of a strength of about 4000 men only about 500 or so, including the Brigade Commander himself and C.O. 39 Baluch with approximately 400 men surrendered to the enemy when he was barely three miles outside Comilla, and as a consequence 53 Bde and all its battalions thus disintegrated;

(v) That he willfully acted in callous disregard of military ethics in abandoning at Laksham 124 sick and wounded with two Medical Officers who were deliberately not informed about the proposed vacation of the fortress; and

(vi) That while vacating the fortress of Laksham he willfully and intentionally abandoned all heavy weapons, stocks of ammunition and supplies for the use of the enemy, without implementing the denial plan;

8. Cases Requiring Departmental Action

(1) Brig. S.A. Ansari, ex-Comd, 23 Bde, (Div)--

This officer assumed command of 23 Bde on the 14th of November 1971 and was responsible for the civil districts of Rangpur and Dinajpur, except the small area of Hilli which was under the control of 205 Bde. Right from the beginning he seems to have been losing ground, starting with the loss of Bhurungamari which was attacked by the

Indians on the 14th or 15th of November 1971. His troops then lost the important position of Pachagarh mainly owing to Brig. Ansari's inability to readjust his position. He then abandoned Thakurgaon between 28th and 30th of November 1971 without offering any resistance to the enemy. As a result of these reverses he was relieved of his command on the 3rd of December 1971. His Divisional Commander, Maj. Gen. Nazar Hussain Shah formed a poor opinion of his performance in battle and we have no hesitation in endorsing the same fro evidence coming before us. We are of the view that he did not display qualities of courage, leadership and determination. The Commission feels that this Officer is not fit for further retention in service.

(2) Brig. Manzoor Ahmad, ex-Comd 57 Bde (9 Div)--

This Officer did not conduct the battle with sufficient grip and caused the loss of fortress of Jhenidah without a fight, owing to his inability to clear an enemy block at Kot Chandpur. Then, contrary to the Divisional concept and without orders he withdrew his Brigade out of the Divisional area and had to be placed under 16 Division. He became detached from his main Headquarters and remained so till the end. He could therefore make no contribution to the war and his performance created the impression that he was shaky in battle. He does not appear to be fit for further retention in service.

(3) Brig. Abdul Qadir Khan, ex-Comd, 93 Bde. (36 Div)--

The work and the conduct of Brig. Abdul Qadir Khan has come to the notice of the Commission in two capacities, namely as the President of the Inter-Services Screening Committee at Dacca and later as Commander of 93 (Ad hoc) Brigade under 36 Division. In the former capacity, he was responsible for the screening of military and civilian personnel as well as non-officials who had either defected during the Awami League movement or had otherwise come to adverse notice. Allegations were made that some persons in his custody were eliminated without trial, or even without any ostensible cause. However, the allegations were not substantiated so as to fix personal responsibility on him. As Commander 93 (Ad hoc) Brigade, he was captured by the Indians while withdrawing to Dacca fro Mymensingh under the orders of Eastern Command. He sees to have reached his ceiling and the Commission formed the impression that his further retention in service would not be in the public interest. We were inferred by the GHQ representative that the Officer had since been retired.

PERFORMANCE OF OTHER SENIOR OFFICERS

9. Besides Lt Gen. A.A.K. Niazi, Maj Gen. Mohammad Jamshed, and Maj Gen M Rahim Khan, with whose cases we have already dealt in the preceding paragraphs, there were four other General Officers serving in the East Pakistan at the time of the surrender, namely, Maj. Gen. M.H. Ansari, GOC 9 Div., Maj. Gen. Qazi Abdul Majid, GOC 14 Div., Maj. Gen. Nazar Hussain Shah, GOC 16 Div., and Maj. Gen. Rao Farman Ali, Adviser to the Governor of East Pakistan. Similarly, besides the Brigadiers, whom we have noticed in the preceding paragraphs, there were 19 other Brigadiers serving in various capacities as Brigade Commanders or Commanders of technical arms. Finally, there was a Rear Admiral of the Navy supported by three Commanders and one Air Commodore commanding the PAF in East Pakistan.

10. While we shall deal with the case of Maj Gen Rao Farman Ali separately, as he was not commanding any troops at the relevant time, we cannot help remarking that

all the senior officers stationed in East Pakistan immediately before and during the war of 1971 must be held collectively responsible for the failings and weaknesses which led to the defeat of the Pakistan Army. However, while assessing their individual responsibility, the Commission was obliged to take note of the limitations imposed on them by the concepts and attitudes adopted by the Eastern Command, the admitted shortages and deficiencies in men and materials, faced by them as compared to the vast resources of the enemy and the general demoralisation which stemmed fro the culpable acts of commission and omission on the part of the Army High Command at Rawalpindi and the Commander Eastern Command, at Dacca. Finally, there was also the unfortunate over-riding factor of a long and inherited tradition of unquestioned obedience and loyalty to the superior commander, which prevented most of these officers from questioning the soundness of the critical decisions and actions taken by the High Command, including the final act of surrender. Apart from a few individuals, the large body of officers and men operating in East Pakistan accepted the final decision without any thought of disobedience, even though the majority of them were undoubtedly willing to fight to the last and lay down their lives for the glory of Pakistan.

11. Keeping in view these factors and circumstances we have examined the individual performance and conduct of these senior officers, as will be apparent from the relevant portions of the Main Report and this Supplement where we have narrated at some length the military events as they developed from day-to-day and we have come to the conclusion that adverse comment reflecting on theory (of) suitability for continued retention in military service would not be justified. We have also not thought it desirable to single out officers for special praise either, although it goes without saying that in several cases the officers did

act with dedication and valour beyond the ordinary call of duty.

PERFORMANCE AND CONDUCT OF JUNIOR OFFICERS

12. In the very nature of things, the Commission was not in a position to examine at any length the conduct and performance of officers below the Brigade level although some cases necessarily came to our notice where the performance of these officers had a direct bearing on the fate of important battles which were fought on various fronts, or where their conduct transgressed the norms of moral discipline. Such cases have found mention in the relevant portions of our report, but by and large cases of these junior officers must be left to be dealt with by the respective Service Headquarters who have ordained detailed briefing reports from all of them and are also in possession of their performance by their immediate superiors.

THE ROLE OF MAJ. GEN. FARMAN ALI

13. Before we conclude this Chapter, brief remarks about the role of Maj. Gen. Farman Ali would not be out of place, for the reason that he has been conspicuously mentioned in several contexts by the international press as well as by the Prime Minister of Bangladesh.

14. This officer remained in East Pakistan continuously from the 28th of February 1967 to the 16th of December 1971. He was Commander, Artillery 14 Div., in the rank of Brigadier from the 28th of February, 1967 to the 25th of March 1969. On the promulgation of Martial Law by General Yahya Khan on the 25th of March 1969 he was appointed as Brigadier (Civil Affairs) in the office of the Zonal Administrator of Martial Law. He was later promoted as Major General in the same post. From the 4th of July 1971 to the 3rd of September 1971 he functioned under the

designation of Maj. Gen. (Political Affairs), and from the latter date to the 14th of December 1971 he worked as Adviser to the Governor of East Pakistan, ceasing to hold this appointment on the resignation of Dr. A.M.Malik.

15. It was inherent in the appointments held by him since the promulgation of General Yahya Khan's Martial Law on the 25th of March 1969 that Maj. Gen. Farman Ali should come into contact with civil officials and political leaders, besides being associated with Army Officers and Martial Law Administrators of various levels and grades. He frankly admitted before the Commission that he was associated with the planning of the military action of the 25th of March 1971, and also with the subsequent political steps taken by the military regime to noramlise the situation, including the proposed by-elections necessitated by the disqualification of a large number of Awami league members of the National and Provincial Assemblies. Nevertheless, as a result of our detailed study of the written statement, submitted by the General and the lengthy cross-examination to which we subjected him during his appearance before us, as well as the evidences from other witnesses from East Pakistan, we have formed the view that Maj. Gen. Farman Ali merely functioned as an intelligent, well-intentioned and sincere staff officer in the various appointments held by him, and at no stage could he be regarded as being a member of the inner military junta surrounding and supporting General Yahya Khan. We have also found that at no stage did he advise, or himself indulge in, actions opposed to public morality, sound political sense or humanitarian considerations. In this context, we have already commented at some length, in a previous Chapter of this Report, on the allegation made by Sheikh Mujibur Rahman at General Farman Ali was wanting to "paint the green of East Pakistan red," and have found that the entire incident has been deliberately distorted.

16. During the critical days of the war this officer had no direct responsibility for military operations, but he was, nevertheless, closely associated with the Governor of East Pakistan as well as the Commander Eastern Command. It was for this reason that he got involved in what has been called "the Farman Ali incident." As we have seen in the chapter dealing with the details of the surrender in East Pakistan, the message authenticated by Maj. Gen. Farman Ali for being dispatched to the United Nations on the 9th of December 1971 had been approved by the Governor of East Pakistan, who had obtained prior authority and clearance from the President of Pakistan, namely, General Yahya Khan, for the purpose of formulating proposals for a settlement and cessation of hostilities in East Pakistan. In these circumstances, the responsibility for its authorship and dispatch could not, therefore, be placed on this officer. In fact, he had, at the time, demanded trial by court martial to clear his position. In view of the facts, as they have now emerged before the Commission, there is no need for any such enquiry or trial.

17. Maj. Gen. Farman Ali was present at Headquarters Eastern Command, during the last phases of the events when Indian Officers came to meet Lt. Gen. Niazi for negotiating the details of the surrender. From the detailed accounts which have come before us of the behaviour and attitude of both these officers, we have no hesitation in recording the opinion that at all relevant times Maj. Gen. Farman Ali advised Lt. Gen. Niazi on correct lines, and if his advice had been accepted, some of the disgraceful episodes might have been avoided.

18. We have also examined the reason why the Indian Commander-in-Chief, General Masnekshaw, addressed certain leaflets to General Farman Ali by describing him as Commander of the Pakistan Army. It appears that on the 8th or 9th December 1971, Lt. Gen. A.A.K. Niazi had not been seen outside his command bunker, and there was

a broadcast by the BBC that he had left East Pakistan and that General Farman Ali had taken over the command of the Pakistan Army. It was for this reason that the Indian Commander addressed General Farman Ali calling upon him to surrender. We are satisfied that at no time did Major General Farman Ali indulge in any communication with the Indian Generals. The situation was in any case rectified when Lt. Gen. Niazi made a public appearance at Hotel Intercontinental, Dacca, before foreign correspondents.

19. An allegation was made before the Commission by Lt. Gen. Niazi that Maj. Gen. Farman Ali had sent out of East Pakistan a large sum of money, approximately Rs 60,000, through his nephew who was a Helicopter Pilot in the Army and left Dacca in the early hours of the 16th of December, 1971. We reported Major General Farman Ali to seek his explanation regarding this allegation and some other matters. He has explained that a sum of Rs 60,000/- had been given by the President of Pakistan to the Governor of East Pakistan for expenditure at his discretion. After the Governor of East Pakistan resigned on or about the 14th December 1971, Maj. Gen. Farman Ali, as Advisor to the Governor, became responsible for this amount. He paid Rs 4000 to Islamia Press, Dacca, and this payment was within the knowledge of the Military Secretary to the Governor, who has also been repatriated to Pakistan. Out of the remaining amount of Rs 56,000/-, Maj. Gen. Farman Ali paid Rs 5000/- to Maj. Gen. Rahim Khan at the time of his evacuation from Dacca on the morning of the 16th of December 1971 to meet the expenses en route which may be required not only by Maj. Gen. Rahim Khan but also by the other persons who were being evacuated with him. It was stated by Maj. Gen. Farman Ali that Maj Gen Rahim Khan had rendered the necessary account of the sum of Rs. 5000/- given to him.

20. After deducting payments made to the Islamia Press, Dacca, and to Maj Gen Rahim Khan an amount of Rs. 51,000/- was left with Maj. Gen. Farman Ali which he physically handed over to his nephew Major Ali Jawaher at the time of his departure from Dacca on the 16th of December 1971. Since his arrival in Pakistan, Maj. Gen. Farman Ali has deposited Rs 46,000/- in the Government Treasury and handed over the treasury receipt to Brig. Qazi, Director Pay and Accounts, GHQ. He has claimed the remaining amount of Rs 5000/- on account of house rent allowance sanctioned by the Government of East Pakistan for the residence of his wife and family in West Pakistan. He has stated the sanctioned allowance was Rs 1400/ PM and the period involved was twelve months, so that he could claim Rs 15000/- but he has claimed only Rs 5000/-.

21. We are satisfied with the explanation rendered by Maj. Gen. Farman Ali, as the facts stated by him are easily verifiable and we do not think that he would have made incorrect statements in this behalf before the Commission.

22. For the foregoing reasons we are of the view that the performance and conduct of Maj. Gen. Farman Ali during the entire period of his service in East Pakistan does not call for any adverse comment.

Chapter 4

CONCLUSIONS

1. This Commission of Inquiry was appointed by the President of Pakistan in Dec. 1971. After examining 213 witnesses, we submitted the Main Report in July, 1972. However, at that time we did not have before us the evidence of the major personalities, except Major General M. Rahim Khan who had played a part in the final events culminating in the surrender in East Pakistan. Accordingly, we stated that "our observations and conclusions regarding the surrender in East Pakistan and other allied matters should be regarded as provisional and subject to modification in the light of the evidence of the Commander, Eastern Command, and other senior officers as and when such evidence becomes available."

2. After the repatriation of prisoners of war from India, the Commission was reactivated in May, 1974. At the resumed session, we have examined as many as 72 persons, including Lt Gen A.A.K. Niazi, Commander, Eastern Command, all the Major Generals and Brigadiers who had served in East Pakistan, Rear Admiral Sharif, Flag Officer

Commanding the Pakistan Navy, Air Commodore Inam, the senior most Air Force Officer, and several civilian officers like the chief Secretary, the Inspector General of Police, two Divisional; Commissioners etc, Maj. Gen. M. Rahim Khan was re-examined at his own request.

3. As it appeared to us that the defeat suffered by the Armed Forces of Pakistan was not merely the result of military factors alone, but had been brought about as the cumulative result of political, international, moral and military factors, we examined all these aspects in our Main Report at some length. We have followed the same pattern of study in the present Supplementary Report. Although we are now naturally in possession of far more detailed information as to the events in East Pakistan, yet the main conclusions reached by us on the earlier occasion have remained unaffected by the fresh evidence now available. In the paragraphs that follow, we intend briefly to summarise our conclusions on these major aspects of the causes of surrender in East Pakistan, making reference, wherever necessary, to the conclusions already embodied in the Main Report.

POLITICAL BACKGROUND

4. In the Main Report, we have traced the genesis of the Pakistan movement, the events preceding the establishment of Pakistan, and the political developments which took place between 1947 and 1971, including a detailed study of the effects of the two Martial Law periods in hastening the process of political and emotional isolation of East Pakistan from West Pakistan.

5. We have also, in the Main Report, examined at length the role played by the two major political parties, namely, the Awami League in East Pakistan and the Pakistan Peoples party in West Pakistan, in bringing about the situation resulting in the postponement of the session of the

73

National Assembly scheduled to be held at Dacca on the 3rd of March, 1971. We have then examined the events occurring between the 1st and the 25th of March, 1971, when the Awami League had seized power from the Government of General Yahya Khan, necessitating resort to the military action of the 25th of March, 1971. We have also touched upon the negotiations which Gen. Yahya Khan was pretending to hold during this period with Sk. Mujibur Rahman on the one hand and political leaders from West Pakistan on the other. Although he never formally declared these negotiations to have failed, yet he secretly left Dacca on the evening of the 25th of March, 1971, leaving instructions behind for military action to be initiated when his plane reached the Karachi area.

6. We have found, as a result of a detailed analysis of the events surrounding the imposition of the second Martial Law by General Yahya Khan on the 25th of March, 1969, that he did not take over the country in order merely to restore normal conditions and reintroduce the democratic process. He did so with a view to obtaining personal power and those who assisted him did so with full knowledge of his intentions. The fresh evidence recorded by us has only served to strengthen this conclusion as to the intentions of Gen. Yahya Khan.

7. All the Senior Army Commanders who were concerned with the administration of Martial Law in East Pakistan as well as the senior civil servants who were inducted into the civil administration in East Pakistan, have expressed the view that military action could not have been a substitute for a political settlement, which was feasible once law and order has been restored within a matter of few weeks after the military action. Most of these witnesses have stated that the most favourable time for a political settlement was between the months of May and September, 1971, during which a reasonable amount of normalcy had been restored and the authority of the Government had been

74

re-established at least in most of the urban areas, if not throughout the countryside. However, no effort was made during these months to start a political dialogue with the elected representatives of the people of East Pakistan; instead fraudulent and useless measures were adopted.

8. The use of excessive force during the military action and the conduct of some of the officers and men of the Pakistan Army during the sweep operations had only served to alienate the sympathies of the people of East Pakistan. The practice of the troops living off the land, in the absence of a proper organisation of their own logistic arrangements during their operations in the countryside, encouraged the troops to indulge in looting. The arbitrary methods adopted by the Martial Law administration in dealing with respectable East Pakistanis, and then sudden disappearances by a process euphemistically called "being sent to Bangladesh" made matters worse. The attitude of the Army authorities towards the Hindu minority also resulted in large-scale exodus to India. The avowed intention of India to dismember Pakistan was only too well known, but even then the need for an early political settlement was not realised by General Yahya Khan. The general amnesty declared by him in August, 1971, proved ineffective, as it was declared too late, and left much to be desired in its implementation. It did not result in the return of any appreciable number of the elected representatives of the people, who were in any case valuable hostages in the hands of the Indian authorities who did not allow them to cross back into Pakistan.

9. Precious moments were thus wasted, during which the Indians mounted their training programme for the Mukti Bahini and started guerrilla raids into Pakistan territory. General Yahya Khan then embarked upon his scheme of by-elections in place of the disqualified Awami League representatives, but these by-elections were an exercise in futility, for the reason that they were supervised and

controlled by the by the Martial Law administration, and even the selection of the candidates was being made by a Major General of the Pakistan Army. In these circumstances, these newly elected representatives did not have any authority to speak on behalf of the people.

10. Similarly, the appointment of Dr. Malik as the civilian Governor of East Pakistan, and the installation of his ministers, did not produce any impact. These gentlemen did not command the confidence of the people, although Dr. Malik was personally respected as a veteran statesman. These attempts at civilization of the Government of East Pakistan were, therefore, an utter failure in winning back the confidence of the people. Power continued to vest in the hands of the Zonal Martial Law Administrator, namely, Lt Gen A.A.K. Niazi. In any case, in view of the circumstances prevailing, namely, the overriding importance of maintaining law and order and keeping the lines of communication open, the role of the army continued to be predominant.

11. Apart, therefore, from the immorality and political expediency of the kind of military action taken by General Yahya Khan on the 25th of March, 1971, it was his culpable failure to arrive at a political settlement with the Awami League during the crucial months preceding the war that completely alienated the sympathies of the population of East Pakistanis, confirming their suspicion that the Generals were not prepared to part with political power in favour of the elected representatives of the people. The refusal of Gen. Yahya Khan to negotiate with the Awami League becomes all the more significant when we remember that two of its top leaders, Sk. Mujibur Rahman and Dr Kamal Hussain were in his custody in West Pakistan, and that almost all the friendly countries had advised him to arrive at a political settlement in view of the looming Indian threat of military action.

12. The two direct and devastating consequences of this political situation brought about by the military regime itself, since holding the elections of 1970, were the prolonged involvement of the Pakistan Army in counter-insurgency measures throughout the Province, and its forced deployment in penny-pockets all along the borders of East Pakistan to prevent infiltration of Mukti Bahini and Indian agents. In the presence of these two factors, the Pakistan Army was obviously fighting a losing battle from the very start.

INTERNATIONAL ASPECT

13. After exhaustively reviewing the state of our international relations as they existed immediately preceding the war, we had expressed the opinion, in the Main Report, that in the background of our relations with India ever since 1947, it should not have been too difficult to appreciate that India would do every thing to precipitate a crisis in East Pakistan.

14. We also took note of the various efforts made by India to internationalise the refugee problem which had arisen as a result of the exodus of people from East Pakistan to India in the wake of the military action. The Indian propaganda was so successful that all efforts made by the military regime in Pakistan to defuse the situation in East Pakistan left the world unimpressed. The situation was further complicated by the mutual assistance treaty signed between India and USSR in Aug, 1971. All the Governments friendly to Pakistan, especially Iran, China and the USA, had made it clear to Gen Yahya that they would not be in a position to render any physical assistance to Pakistan in the event of an armed conflict with India. However, the significance of this international situation was unfortunately completely lost on Gen Yahya Khan and his

associates. They blundered ahead, oblivious of the fatal consequences of their international isolation.

15. In the Main Report we also dealt with the activities at the United Nations during the critical days of the war, and came to the conclusion that there was no rational explanation why Gen Yahya Khan did not take the dispute to the Security Council immediately after the Indian invasion of East Pakistan on the 21st of November, 1971, nor was it possible to explain his refusal to accept the first Russian Resolution, if indeed the situation in East Pakistan had become militarily so critical that surrender was inevitable. In this context we also referred to the message which was handed over by Major General Farman Ali to Mr. Paul Mure Henry, Representative of the UN at Dacca for onward transmission to the Secretary General of the UN, offering certain proposals for a political settlement in East Pakistan. Finally, we expressed the opinion that if Gen Yahya Khan as Commander-in-Chief of the Army had shown greater determination and courage and directed the Eastern Command to hold on somewhat longer than the 16th of December, 1971, it was quite possible that a satisfactory solution ordering a cease-fire might have been obtained from the Security Council.

16. During the present phase of our enquiry nothing has been said by the witnesses about the state of our international relations and their impact on the 1971 war, nor about the moves in the United Nations except that Major Gen Farman Ali has clarified the position with regard to the message attributed to him. He had stated that the message was drafted under the instructions of the Governor of East Pakistan who had been authorised by the President of Pakistan to offer proposals for a political settlement with the Awami League, and that he handed over a copy of the same to Mr. Paul Mure Henry as directed by the Governor of East Pakistan. While this clarification removes the mystery surrounding the so-called "Farman

Ali incident," it does not in any manner affect the conclusions already stated by us in the main Report as regards the international aspect.

THE MILITARY ASPECT

17. While discussing the military aspect of the war in the Main Report we came to the conclusion that the major role in the 1971 disaster had been that of the ground forces, that the strategic concept embodied in war Directive No.4 of 1967, required a drastic revision in the light of the political and military situation developing as a result of the military action in East Pakistan in March 1971, but the Army High Command did not carry out any study in depth of the effect of these new factors, nor did it pay any attention to the growing disparity between the war preparedness and the capability of the armed forces of Pakistan and India as a result of the Indo-Soviet Treaty of Aug 1971. We dealt at length with the concepts of defence as well as the plans formulated by the General Headquarters both for East and West Pakistan, and pointed out the defects and deficiencies in those plans, apart from the inadequacy of resources available on both fronts as compared to those of the enemy. However, we observed that our study of the military aspect of the war in East Pakistan, both limited and total, was inconclusive on account of the non-availability of the evidence of the Commander, Eastern Command, and other senior officers then serving in East Pakistan.

18. Having now had the advantage of examining these commanders at considerable length we feel we are in a position to formulate our final conclusions as to the causes of surrender in East Pakistan.

19. There has been some controversy as to the exact status of Lt Gen. A.A.K. Niazi, namely, whether he was a Theatre Commander or merely a Corps Commander, al-

though he has been officially described as Commander, Eastern Command. While a Corps Commander is merely a Commander of a number of divisions placed under his command, a Theatre Commander is not merely in command of all the forces in the area, including the Naval and the Air Forces. In case of East Pakistan the Flag Officer Commanding of the Navy and the Air Force Commanding of the Pakistan Air Force were directly under their own respective Commanders-in-chief, although they were instructed to liaise and coordinate with the Commander, Eastern Command. Technically speaking, therefore, Lt. Gen. Niazi was not a Theatre Commander and was never designated as such. Nevertheless, situated as he was, we consider that at least from the 3rd of Dec 1971 onwards, on which date war broke out on the Western Front as well, Lt Gen Niazi became, for all intents and purposes, an independent Corps Commander, possessing of necessity and by force of circumstances all the powers of a Theatre Commander, and even the General Headquarters expected him to act as such, for there was no possibility thereafter of replacing him by another Commander of equivalent rank. General Niazi's conduct of war , as also his final decision to surrender, have, therefore, to be judged in this light.

20. The traditional concept of defence adopted by Pakistan Army was that the defence of East Pakistan lies in West Pakistan. However Lt. Gen. Niazi contented before the Commission that the Indians would not have started an all-out war in East Pakistan if the Western Front had not been opened by Pakistan. It seems to us that this contention is based on a lack of proper appreciation of the enemy threat which was fast developing in the Eastern Theatre. It had become quite evident that the Mukti Bahini, on their own , even after their training in India would never be able to face a pitched battle with the Pakistan Army, and the Indians could not afford to prolong the war by proxy for an indefinite period. The plan of capturing a sizable

chunk of territory for setting up Bangladesh has also been frustrated by the forward deployment of our troops. An all-out war had, therefore, become inevitable for India, and in such an event the only course open for Pakistan was to implement the traditional concept of defending East Pakistan from West Pakistan in an determined and effective manner. The concept, therefore, that the defence of East Pakistan lies in West Pakistan remained valid and if ever there was need to invoke this concept it was on the 21st of Nov. 1971 when the Indian troops had crossed the East Pakistan borders in naked aggression. Unfortunately, the delay in opening the Western front and the half-hearted and hesitant manner in which it was ultimately opened only helped in precipitating the catastrophe in East Pakistan.

21. The Operational instructions issued by the Eastern Command as No. 3 of 1971 on the 15th of July 1971, contemplated a forward defensive posture with strong points and fortresses which were to be made logistically self-sufficient to fight a battle lasting for at least 30 days, even if by-passed. They were also expected to act as firm bases or jumping-off points for actions against the enemy from the flanks or from behind. Dacca was to be defended at all costs by being made into a fortress, as it was the lynch-pin, both politically and militarily.

22. The plan envisaged as many as 25 fortresses and 9 strong points, consisting mainly of built up areas such as district or sub-divisional headquarters towns, large villages and cantonments. The paucity of troops did not permit them to be manned but it was expected that the troops deployed along the border and in counter insurgency operations would gradually fall back and take up defensive positions within the fortresses and strong points. His concept further contemplated that the fortresses would be defended to the last man and last round.

23. The fortress concept postulates 3 essential conditions for its success namely :

(a). That there must be adequate reserves to strike the enemy if bypasses the fortress, and to give mutual support to another fortress;

(b). That the fortress must be so located as to be able to mutually support each other and

(c). That the population in the areas in which such fortresses are located is not hostile. Gen. Niazi was fully aware that none of these conditions were fulfilled in East Pakistan as he did not have enough troops to man 34 fortress and strong points with his then 29 battalions; his fortress and strong points were so located that they were not in a position to mutually support each other, and he also knew that the local population was hostile and movement of his troops would be made impossible by the Mukti Bahini. We are at a loss to understand how he expected the concept to succeed in these circumstances.

24. The evidence clearly discloses that none of the fortresses were manned nor did they have protective defences capable of withstanding enemy attacks supported by armour. Troops were expected to man these fortresses after falling back from their forward: even such artillery or heavy weapons as the troops possessed were to the fortresses. The withdrawal of the troops to the fortresses was as was to be expected in these circumstances, by no means an orderly withdrawal , but in most cases it was a disorderly retreat, leaving even the heavy equipment behind. There were no reserves with any local Commanders, except for 16 Division, and the command reserve of only a brigade strength and also been committed in the Eastern sector, through which the main enemy thrust came. This soundness of the fortress concept thus stood thoroughly exposed by the end which it produced.

25. In our view, the concept was utterly inappropriate for achieving the mission assigned to the Commander, Eastern Command, of defending East Pakistan and maintaining his presence in East Pakistan in the changed situation created by the war launched by the enemy. The wisest course of action for Gen. Niazi would have been to concentrate his troops in a smaller area, protected by the major natural obstacles around the military and political lynch pin - Dacca.

26. At any rate, there should have been a contingency plan for a planned withdrawal into thew Dacca triangle to cater for fighting a all-out war with an enemy vastly superior in resources and capabilities both on the ground and in the air. The failure on part of the Eastern Command to so plan amounts to gross negligence for, in fact , what was done was merely to give battle in weakness and be forced to retreat in disorder. The fortress strategy might have been suitable for carrying out the counter insurgency operations, but after the 21st of Nov. 1971, it became redundant. The net result of this strategy was to give the opposite advantage to the enemy, who at his leisure routed and dispersed our troops while himself concentratingly advanced in order towards Dacca.

27. The tragedy with Gen Niazi has been his obsession that he will not be called upon to fight any major battles with the Indians in East Pakistan, in spite of enormous Indian buildup around East Pakistan, the detailed briefing given by GHQ to his Chief of Staff about the Indian plans and the advice given to him by the chief of the General Staff and the Vice-chief of the General Staff, during their last visit to the Eastern Theatre, for the deployment of his troops. Gen. Niazi's only reaction to these warnings about the new threat was to hastily raise two ad hoc Divisions namely 36 Div in Sept. 1971 and 39 Div on the 19th of Nov. 1971 by committing his command reserves.

28. Lt Gen Niazi tried to justify the deployment of his reserves by saying that he had been promised 8 more battalions, and if these had been sent, he would have had enough troops to create a command reserve as also to meet then deficiencies of the new ad hoc formations. The evidence unfortunately does not disclose that any firm commitment was made by GHQ. We also find that even if the extra battalions had been sent the position would not have materially improved as there was no clear plan for their deployment. Gen. Niazi was therefore not justified in denuding himself of his reserves before the actual arrival of the additional troops.

29. We are also not impressed by the excuse put forward by the Commander, Eastern Command for not modifying his plans, namely that the mission originally assigned to him hold every inch of territory in East Pakistan and to prevent the establishment of Bangladesh by the capture of any sizeable chunk of territory, was never changed by the High Command. As an independent Corps Commander, thousands of miles away from the GHQ, it should have been apparent to him that at least from the 21 Nov. 1971 onwards the more important part of his mission was to defend East Pakistan and to keep the Corps in being, by giving up territory if necessary.

30. We also find that it is not correct to say that the mission given to the Eastern Command was never changed, because the GHQ had given him through more than one message a clear indication that territory had become less important, and that the Command should fight for time keeping in view only territories of strategic importance.

31. The detailed narrative of events as given by us in the Supplementary Report, clearly shows that the planning was hopelessly defective and there was no plan at all for the defence of Dacca, nor for any concerted effort to stem the enemy onslaught with a Division or a Brigade battle at any

stage. It was only when the general found himself gradually being encircled by the enemy which had successfully managed to bypass his fortresses and reached Faridpur , Khulna, Daudkandi and Chandpur (the shortest route to Dacca) that he began to make frantic efforts to get the troops back for the defence of Dacca. It was unfortunate then too late, the ferries necessary for crossing the troops over the big Jamuna river from the area of 16 division had disappeared and the Mukti Bahini had invested the area behind, making vehicular movement impossible. Orderly withdrawal of troops in time for concentrated defence was also made impossible by the unfortunate orders issued by Lt. Gen. Niazi that no withdrawal was to take place unless cleared two up and without suffering 75% casualties.

32. In the absence of contingency plans for the withdrawal of troops into the Dacca triangle area behind the big rivers , to prevent the enemy breakthrough and to deal if need be with the known capability of the enemy to heli-drop troops behind our lines after it had acquired mastery of the air by either eliminating or neutralising our Air Force of only one squadron, it was not at all a matter of surprise that the defences should have collapsed immediately in thin lines in the forward positions were pierced by the enemy. On the fourth day of the all-out-war major fortresses were abandoned without a fight, namely, Jessore and Jhenidah the West and the Brahmanbaria in the East. On the next day the Comilla fortress was isolated by encirclement from all sides, and on the 9th of Dec 1971, even a divisional commander abandoned his area of responsibility with his headquarters, leaving his formation behind. On the same day 2 more fortresses Kushtia and Laksham were abandoned. At the latter fortress even the sick and the wounded were left behind. By 10 Dec 1971, even Hilli, where a determined battle had been fought for 16 days had to be abandoned. The Brigade returning from Mymensingh got entangled with heli dropped Indian troops, and the

Brigade Commander and some of his troops were taken prisoner.

THE SURRENDER

33. The painful story of the last few days immediately preceding the surrender on 16 dec 1971 has been narrated in Part V of the Supplementary Report. We have come to the conclusion that there was no order to surrender, but in view of the desperate picture painted by the Commander, Eastern Command, the higher authorities only gave him permission to surrender if he in his judgement thought it was necessary. Gen Niazi, could have disobeyed such an order if he thought he had the capability of defending Dacca. On his own estimate, he had 26,400 men at Dacca in uniform and he could have held out for at least another 2 weeks, because the enemy would have taken a week to build up its forces in the Dacca area and another week to reduce the fortress of Dacca. If Gen. Niazi had done so and lost his life in the process, he would have made history and would have been remembered by the coming generations as a great hero and a martyr, but the events show that he had already lost the will to fight after the 7th December 1971, when his major fortresses at Jessore and Brahmanbaria had fallen. The question of creating history, therefore, was never in his mind.

34. Even more painful than the military failures of lt. Gen Niazi is the story of the abject manner in which he agreed to sign the surrender document laying down arms to the so-called joint-command of India and Mukti Bahini, to be present at the Airport to receive the victorious Indian General Aurora, to present a guard of honour to the Indian General, and then to participate in the public surrender ceremony at the Race Course, to the everlasting shame of Pakistan and its Armed forces. Even if he had been obliged to surrender, by force of circumstances, it was not

86

necessary for him to behave in this shameful manner at every step of the process of surrender. The detailed accounts which have been given before the commission by those who had the misfortune of witnessing these events, leave no doubt that Lt. Gen. Niazi had suffered a complete moral collapse during the closing phases of the war.

35. While undoubtedly the responsibility for these failures lies with the Commander, Eastern Command, GHQ cannot escape its responsibility, as the plan had been approved by it. It was also the responsibility of GHQ to correct the mistakes of the Eastern Command, as communications were open to the last. It was incumbent upon GHQ to guide, direct and influence the conduct of the war in the Eastern Theatre, if the Commander himself in that Theatre was incapable of doing so. But the GHQ failed in this important duty. The Commander-in-Chief remained indifferent.

36. While we have not specially condemned the performance of senior Officers other than Lt. Gen. A.A..K. Niazi, Maj. Gen. Mohammad Jamshed, Maj. Gen. M. Rahim Khan and some of the Brigadiers, we cannot help remarking that all the Senior Officers stationed in East Pakistan immediately before and during the war of 1997 must be held collectively responsible for the failings and weaknesses which led to the defeat of the Pakistan Army. The only thing which goes in their favour is that while assessing their individual responsibility the Commission was obliged to take note of the limitations imposed upon them by the concepts and attitudes adopted by the Eastern Command, the admitted shortages and deficiencies in men and materials faced by them as compared to the vast resources of the enemy, and the general demoralization which stemmed from the culpable acts of commission and omission on the part of the Army High Command at Rawalpindi and the Commander, Eastern Command at Dacca. Finally, there was also the unfortunate overriding

factor of a long and inherited tradition of unquestioned obedience and loyalty to the superior Commander which prevented most of these Officers from questioning the soundness of the critical decisions and actions taken by the High Command, including the final act of surrender.

37. Before we conclude this part of the discussion, we would like to place on record that, apart from a few individuals, the large body of officers and men operating in East Pakistan accepted the final decision without any thought of disobedience only owing to their ingrained sense of discipline, and the majority of them would have been undoubtedly willing to fight to the last and lay down their lives for the glory of Pakistan. The gallantry and determination with which some of the battles were fought in East Pakistan has been acknowledged even by the enemy.

PROFESSIONAL RESPONSIBILITY OF CERTAIN SENIOR ARMY COMMANDERS

40. From the conclusions outlined by us in the preceding paragraphs, particularly as regards the military aspect of the debacle it was have become clear that in our view several senior Army Commanders have been guilty of serious dereliction of duty in formulating and executing the defence plans, and since are even guilty of shamefully abandoning the fortresses which it was their duty to defend. We have also found that the Commander, Eastern Command, and his chief of Staff, Brig. Baqir Siddiqui displayed willful neglect in the matter of the execution of denial plans, with the result that large quantities of valuable war materials, equipment, installations, arms and ammunition were delivered intact to the Indians at the time of surrender. All these acts of omission and commission call for deterrent action by way of court materials wherever permissible under the law. Detailed recommendations in respect of all these matters are contained in the next Chapter.

41. It has come to the notice of the Commission that during his period of captivity, and even after repatriation to Pakistan, Lt. Gen. A.A.K. Niazi assisted by his Chief of Staff, Brig. Baqir Siddiqui, has been making efforts to influence his Divisional and Brigade Commanders, by threats and inducements, so as to persuade them to present a coordinated story of the events in East Pakistan with a view to mitigating his own responsibility for the debacle. This is a serious matter and calls for notice.

42. The surrender in East Pakistan has indeed been a tragic blow to the nation. By the act of surrender Pakistan stood dismembered, and the image of the Pakistan Army as an efficient and excellent fighting force stood shattered. We can only hope that the nation has learnt the necessary lessons from these tragic events and that effective and early action will be taken in the light of the conclusions reached in the report.

Chapter 5

RECOMMENDATIONS

In the concluding portion of our Main Report, submitted in 1972, we had made a number of recommendations based on our study of the various aspects of the causes of the debacle of 1971. Some of these recommendations need to be modified, or amplified, in the light of the fresh evidence which we have now recorded; while the need for the others has only been further emphasised. We believe that the object of setting up this Commission would be fully realised only of appropriate and early action is taken by the Government on these recommendation.

2. Even though it involves a repetition of what we have already said in the Main Report, we consider that it would be appropriate if all our recommendations are now finally set out at one place, for facility of reference and action. Detailed reasons and justification for these recommendations will be found in the relevant Chapters of the Main Report as well as this Supplementary Report. We are aware that some of these recommendations have already

been implemented, but this would not appear to be a reason for not including them in this final summing up.

TRIALS

3. There is consensus on the imperative need of bringing to book those senior Army Commanders who have brought disgrace and defeat to Pakistan by their subversion of the Constitution, usurpation of political power by criminal conspiracy, their professional incompetence, culpable negligence and wilful neglect in the performance of their duties and physical and moral cowardice in abandoning the fight when they had the capability and resources to resist the enemy. Firm and proper action would not only satisfy the nation's demand for punishment where it is deserved, but would also ensure against any future recurrence of the kind of shameful conduct displayed during the 1971 war. We accordingly recommend that the following trials be undertaken without delay. : -

(i) That General Yahya Khan, General Abdul Hamid Khan, Lt. Gen. S.G.M.M. Pirzada, Lt. Gen. Gul Hasan, Maj. Gen. Umar and Maj. Gen. Mitha should be publicly tried for being party to a criminal conspiracy to illegally usurp power from F.M. Mohammad Ayub Khan in power if necessary by the use of force. In furtherance of their common purpose they did actually try to influence political parties by threats, inducements and even bribes to support their designs both for bringing about a particular kind of result during the elections of 1970, and later persuading some of the political parties and the elected members of the National Assembly to refuse to attend the session of the National Assembly scheduled to be held at Dacca on the 3rd of March, 1971. They, furthermore, in agreement with each other brought about a situation in East Pakistan which led to a civil disobedience movement, armed revolt by the Awami League and subsequently tot he surrender of our troops in East Pakistan and the dismemberment of Pakistan:

(ii) That the Officers mentioned in No. (i) above should also be tried for criminal neglect of duty in the conduct of war both in East Pakistan and West Pakistan. The details of this neglect would be found in the Chapters dealing with the military aspect of the war

(iii) That Lt. Gen. Irshad Ahmad Khan, former Commander 1 Corps, be tried for criminal and wilful neglect of duty in conducting the operations of his Corps in such a manner that nearly 500 villages of the Shakargarh tehsil of Sialkot district in West Pakistan were surrendered to the enemy without a fight and as a consequence the Army offensive in the south was seriously jeopardised;

(iv) That Maj. Gen. Abid Zahid, former GOC 15 Div, be tried for wilful neglect of duty and shameful surrender of a large area comprising nearly 98 villages in the Phuklian salient in the Sialkot district of West Pakistan, which surrender also posed a standing threat to the safety of Marala Headworks by bringing the Indian forces within nearly 1500 yards thereof. He also kept the GHQ in the dark about Indian occupation of the Phuklian salient until the loss was discovered after the war.

(v) That Maj. Gen B.M. Mustafa, former GOC 18 Division, be tried for wilful neglect of duty in that his offensive plan aimed at the capture of the Indian position of Ramgarh in the Rajasthan area (Western Front) was militarily unsound and haphazardly planned, and its execution resulted in severe loss of vehicles and equipment in the desert.

(vi) That Lt. Gen. A.A.K. Niazi, former Commander, Eastern Command, be court-martialed on 15 charges as set out in Chapter III of part V of the Supplementary Report regarding his wilful neglect in the performance of his professional and military duties connected with the defence of East Pakistan and the shameful surrender of his forces tot he Indians at a juncture when he still had the capability and resources to offer resistance.

(vii) That Maj. Gen. Mohammad Jamshed, former GOC 36 (ad-hoc) Division, Dacca, be tried by court martial on five charges listed against him, in the aforementioned part of the Supplementary Report, for wilful neglect of his duty in the preparation of plans for the defence of Dacca and showing complete lack of courage and will to fight, in acquiescing in the decision of the Commander, Eastern Command, to surrender to the Indian forces when it was still possible to put up resistance for a period of two weeks or so, and also for willfully neglecting to inform the authorities concerned, on repatriation to Pakistan, about the fact of distribution of Rs. 50,000 by him out of Pakistan currency notes and other funds at his disposal or under his control in East Pakistan.

(viii) That Maj. Gen. M. Rahim Khan, former GOC 39 (ad-hoc) Division, Chandpur, in East Pakistan, be tried by court martial on five charges listed against him in this Report for showing undue regard for his personal safety in abandoning his Division, his Divisional troops and area of responsibility and vacating his Divisional Headquarters from Chandpur on the 8th of December, 1971; for his wilful insistence on moving by day owing to fear of Mukti Bahini and thus causing the death of fourteen Naval ratings and four Officers of his own HQ, besides injuries to himself and several others, due to strafing by Indian aircraft; for his abandoning valuable signal equipment at Chandpur; for spreading despondency and alarm by certain conversation on the 12th of December, 1971, at Dacca; and for willfully avoiding submitting a debriefing report to GHQ on being specially evacuated to West Pakistan in early 1971 so as to conceal the circumstances of his desertion from him Divisional Headquarters at Chandpur.

(ix) That Brig. G.M. Baquir Siddiqui, former GOS, Eastern Command, Dacca, be tried by court martial on nine charges as formulated in this Report, for his wilful neglect of duty in advising the Commander, Eastern Command, as regards the concept and formulation of defence plans, appreciation of the Indian threat, execution of denial plans, abrupt changes in command, friendliness with he Indian during captivity and attempts to influence formation Commanders by threats and inducements to present a coordinated story before the GHQ and the Commission of Inquiry in regard to the events leading to surrender in East Pakistan.

(x) That Brig Mohammad Hayat, former Commander 107 Brigade, 9 Division, East Pakistan, be tried by court martial on four charges for displaying wilful neglect in not formulating a sound plan for the defence of the fortress of Jessore; for failing to properly plan and command the brigade counter-attack at Gharibpur, for shamefully abandoning the fortress of Jessore and delivering intact to the enemy all supplies and ammunition dumps; and disobeying the orders of the GOC 9 Division, to withdraw to Magura in the event of a forced withdrawal from Jessore;

(xi) That Brig Mohammad Aslam Niazi, former commander 53 Brigade, 39 (ad-hoc) Division, East Pakistan, be tried by court martial on six charges for displaying culpable lack of initiative, determination and planning ability in that he failed to occupy and prepare defences at Mudafarganj as ordered by his GOC on the 4th of December, 1971; for failing to eject the enemy from Mudafarganj as ordered on the 6th of December, 1971; for shamefully abandoning the fortress of Laksham on or about the 9th of December, 1971; for wilful neglect in failing to properly organise exfiltration of his troops from the fortress of Laksham to Comilla on the 9th of December, 1971, thus resulting in heavy casualties and capture of several elements of his troops on the way; for showing callous disregard of military ethics in abandoning at Laksham 124 sick and wounded with two Medical Officers without informing them about the proposed vacation of the fortress; and for abandoning intact at Laksham all heavy weapons, stocks of ammunition and supplies for the use of the enemy

II. INQUIRY AND TRIALS FOR ALLEGED ATROCITIES

4. That as recommended in Paragraph 7 of Chapter III of Part V of the Main Report and in Paragraph 39 of Chapter II of Part V of this Supplementary Report, a high-powered Court or Commission of Inquiry be set up to investigate into persistent allegations of atrocities said to have been committed by the Pakistan Army in East Pakistan during its operations from March to December, 1971, and to hold trials of those who indulged in these atrocities, brought a bad name to the Pakistan Army and alienated the sympathies of the local population by their acts of wanton cruelty and immorality against our own people. The composition of the Court of Inquiry, if not its proceedings, should be publicly announced so as to satisfy national conscience and international opinion. The Commission feels that sufficient evidence is now available in Pakistan for a fruitful inquiry to be undertaken in this regard. As the Government of Bangladesh has since been recognised by Pakistan, it may also be feasible to request the Dacca authorities to forward to this Court of Inquiry whatever evidence may be available with them.

III. OTHER INQUIRIES

5 . (i) That allegations of personal immorality, drunkenness and indulgence in corrupt practices against General Yahya Khan, General Abdul Hamid Khan and Maj. Gen Khuda Dad Khan be properly investigated as there is prima facie evidence to show that their moral degeneration resulted in indecision, cowardice and professional incom-

petence. In the light of the result of this inquiry suitable charges may be added against these Officers, during the trials we have already recommended earlier. The details of the allegations and the evidence relating thereto will be found in Chapter I of Part V of the Main Report.

(ii) That similar allegations of personal immorality, acquiring a notorious reputation in this behalf at Sialkot, Lahore and Dacca, and indulgence in the smuggling of Pan from East to West Pakistan made against Lt. Gen. Niazi should also be inquired into and, if necessary, made the subject matter of additional charges at the trial earlier recommended in respect of the performance of his professional duties in East Pakistan. The details of these allegations and the evidence relating thereto will be found in Chapter I of Part V of the Main Report and in Chapter I of part V of this supplementary Report.

(iii) That an inquiry is also indicated into the disposal of Rs. 50,000 said to have been distributed by Maj. Gen. Mohammad Jamshed, former GOC 39 (ad-hoc) Division and Director General, East Pakistan Civil Armed Forces immediately before the surrender on the 16th of December 1971. Details of this matter including the General's explanation would be found in paragraphs 21 to 23 of Chapter I of Part V of the Supplementary Report. We have already recommended that this Officer be tried by a court martial on several charges including his wilful failure to disclose any facts at all about his sum Rs. 50,000. That charge does not necessarily imply any dishonest practice on his part. The inquiry now suggested can form a part of the charges already recommended.

(iv) That allegations of indulging in large-scale looting of property in East Pakistan including theft of Rs. 1, 35,00,000 from the National Bank Treasury at Siraj Ganj persistently made against Brig. Jehanazeb Arbab, former Commander 57 Brigade, Lt Col (now Brig) Muzaffar Ali

Zahid, former CO 31 Field Regiment, Lt. Col. Basharat Ahmad, former CO 18 Punjab, Lt. Col Mohammad Taj, former CO 32 Punjab, Lt Col Mohammad Tufail, former CO 55 Field Regiment and Major Madad Hussain Shah of 18 Punjab, as set out in paragraph 24 and 25 of Chapter I of part V of the Supplementary Report, should be thoroughly inquired into and suitable action taken in the light of the proved facts.

(v) That an inquiry be held into the allegation, noticed by us in paragraph 36 of Chapter 1 of Part V of the Main Report, that while serving in the Martial Law Administration at Multan, Maj. Gen. Jahanzeb, presumably a Brigadier at that time, demanded a bribe of Rs. One lac from a PCS Officer posted as Chairman of the Municipal Committee of Multan, on pain of proceeding against him for corruption under martial Law, as a consequence of which demand the said PCS Officer is said to have committed suicide leaving behind a letter saying that although he had made only Rs.15,000 he was being required to pay Rs. one lac to the Martial Law officers. The allegation was made before the Commission by Brig. Mohammad Abbas Beg (Witness No.9)

(vi) That in inquiry is also necessary into the allegation made against Brig. Hayatullah that he entertained some women in his bunker in the Maqbulpur sector (West Pakistan) on the night of the 11th or 12th of December, 1971, when Indian shells were falling on his troops. The allegation was contained in an anonymous letter addressed to the Commission and supported in evidence before us by the Brigadier Hayatullah's brigade, Major, namely, Major Munawar Khan (Witness No.42).

(vii) That it is necessary to investigate into the allegations, as set out in Paragraphs 9 to 14 of Chapter 1 of Part V of the Main Report, to the effect that senior Army Commanders grossly abused their official position and powers under the Martial Law to acquire large allotments of land, and obtained substantial house buildings loans on extremely generous terms from certain banking institutions with which they deposited large amounts from departmental funds entrusted to their care. Those found guilty of corrupt practices should receive the punishment they deserve under the military law or the ordinary criminal law of the land as the case may be.

(viii) That a thorough investigation be conducted into the suspicion created in the mind of the Commission, during the recording of additional evidence of Officers repatriated form India, that there may be some complicity or collusion between the Commander, Easter Command (Lt. Gen. A.A.K. Niazi) and his Chief of Staff (Brig G.M. Baqir Saddiqui) on the one hand and the Indian authorities on the other in the matter of the failure of the Pakistan Armed Forces to carry out execution of denial plans immediately before the surrender in spite of instructions issued in this behalf by GHQ on the 10th of December, 1971. We have already included relevant charges in this behalf against these two Officers, but we consider that it would be in the public interest to depute a specialized agency to probe into the matter further. On the material available to us we cannot put the matter higher than suspicion, but we have not been able to find any reasonable, or even plausible explanation for the orders issued by the Easter Command to stop the execution of denial plans, particularly in Dacca and Chittagong, thus ensuring the delivery intact to the Indians of large amounts of war materials and other equipment. Details of these deliveries will be found in our Chapter VII of Part IV dealing with the aftermath of surrender.

(ix) That an inquiry be held into the circumstances under which Commander Gul Zareen of the Pakistan Navy was carried from Khulna to Singapore on the 7th of December, 1971, by a French ship called M.V. Fortescue, thus abandoning his duties at PNS Titumir Naval Base, Khulna. The

case of this Officer was dealt with by us in Paragraphs 12
and 13 of Chapter III of Part V of the Main Report.

IV. CASES REQUIRING DEPARTMENTAL ACTION

6. While examining the course of events and the conduct
of war in East Pakistan, we formed a poor opinion about
the performance and capabilities of Brig. S.A .Ansari, ex-
Commander 23 Brigade, Brig. Manzoor Ahmad, ex-Commander 57 Brigade, 9 Division, and Brig. Abdul Qadir
Khan, ex-Commander 94 brigade, 36 (ad hoc) Division.
We consider that their further retention in service is not in
the public interest and they may accordingly be retired.

V. PERFORMANCE AND CONDUCT OF JUNIOR OFFICERS

7. In the very nature of things the Commission was not
in a position to examine at any length the conduct and
performance of officers below the brigade level, although
some case necessarily came to our notice where the performance of these Officers had a direct bearing on the fate
of important battles or where their conduct transgressed
the norms of discipline. Such cases have been mentioned
by us at their proper place, but by and large cases of junior
officers must be dealt with by the respective service headquarters who have obtained detailed debriefing reports
from all of them and are also in possession of the assess-
ment of their performance by their immediate superiors.

VI. MEASURES FOR MORAL REFORM IN THE ARMED FORCES

8. While dealing at some length with the moral aspect of
the 1971 debacle, in Chapter I of Part V of the Main Report as well as in the corresponding Chapter of the present Supplementary Report, we have expressed the opinion
that there is indeed substance in the widespread allegation, rather belief, that due to corruption arising out of

the performance of Martial Law duties, lust for wine and women, and greed for lands and houses a large number of senior Army Officers, particularly those occupying the highest positions, had not only lost the will to fight but also the professional competence necessary for taking the vital and critical decisions demanded of them for the successful prosecution of the war. Accordingly, we recommend that: -

(i) The Government should call upon all Officers of the Armed Forces to submit declarations of their assets, both moveable and immovable, and those acquired in the names of their relations and dependents during the last ten years (they were exempted from submitting such declarations during the last two periods of martial Law). If on examination of such declarations any Officer is found to have acquired assets beyond this known means, then appropriate action should be taken against him

(ii) The Armed Services should devise ways and means to ensure: -

(a) That moral values are not allowed to be compromised by infamous behaviour particularly at higher levels;

(b) That moral rectitude is given due weight along with professional qualities in the matter of promotion to higher ranks;

(c) That syllabi of academic studies at the military academics and other Service Institutions should include courses designed to inculcate in the young minds respect for religious democratic and political institutions;

(d) That use of alcoholic drinks should be banned in military messes and functions

(e) That serious notice should be taken of notorious sexual behaviour and other corrupt practices

VII. DISCIPLINE AND TERMS AND CONDITIONS OF SERVICE

9. These matters were discussed by us in Chapter III of Part V of the Main Report, and for the reasons given therein we make the following recommendations: -

(i) An inter-services study should be undertaken of the operative terms and conditions of service and amenities available to Officers, JCOs and other ranks of the Services so as to remove disparities existing in this behalf and causing discontentment among the junior officers and other ranks of various Services

(ii) The GHQ should consider the advisability of adopting recommendations contained in the report submitted by the Discipline Committee headed by the late Maj. Gen. Iftikhar Khan Janjua

(iii) The Navy and Air Force might also appoint their own Discipline Committees to consider the peculiar problems of their Services, such measure to be in addition to the inter-services study recommended above.

VIII. IMPROVEMENT AND MODERNIZATION OF THE PAKISTAN NAVY

10. From the detailed discussion of the role of the Navy, as contained in Section (D) of Chapter VIII of Part IV of the Main Report, and supplemented by further details of its operations in East Pakistan is set out in this Supplementary Report, it seems to us that the following steps are urgently called for to improve our naval capability: -

(i) That immediate attention should be given to he basic requirements for the modernization of the Pakistan Navy in order to make it capable of protecting the only sea port of Pakistan and of keeping the lifelines of the nation open. The Navy has been sadly neglected ever since the first Martial Law regime, for in the concept of Army Commander the Navy was not expected to play much of a role. The folly of this theory was fully demonstrated during this war. The Pakistan Navy, we strongly recommend, should have its own air arm of suitable aircraft for the purpose of reconnaissance and for defence against missile boats. This is the only way in which the threat posed by the growing Indian Navy and her missile boats can be countered.

(ii) There is urgent need for developing a separate harbour for the Navy away from Karachi, from where the Navy can protect the approaches to Karachi more effectively

(iii) In view of the serious handicaps which were posed by the late conveyance of the D-day and the H-hour to the Pakistan Navy and its total exclusion from he planning for war, the need for making the Navy a fully operative member in he joint Chiefs of Staff Organization is imperative.

IX. Improvement in the Role of P.A.F.

11. In Section (C) of Chapter VIII of Part IV of the Main Report as well as in a separate Chapter of the present supplement (viz Chapter X of Part III), we have discussed at length the role and performance of the P.A.F. in the 1971 war. In the light of that discussion, we recommend as follows: -

(i) We are not convinced that a more forward-looking posture cannot be adopted by the Air Force having regard to the peculiar needs of the country. We recommend, therefore, that Pakistan should have more forward air fields located at such places from where it might be in a position to give more protection to our vital line of communication as well as to major centres of industry. The adoption of such a forward strategy would also increase the striking capabilities of our fighters.

(ii) There is need also to improve the working of our early warning system. The time lag between the observation of an enemy aircraft by the first line of Mobile Observer Units and the final collation of that information in the Air Operation Centre takes unduly long because of the draftory system of reporting adopted. Training exercises to co-ordinate the working of the various agencies employed for the operation of the early warning system should be held periodically to keep them at a high pitch of efficiency.

(iii) The Karachi Port should also be provided as soon as possible, with a low level seaward-looking radar which it seriously lacks and due to the want of which it suffered many handicaps during the last war.

(iv) That with the increased Indian capability of blockading Karachi with missile boats the air defence of Karachi should be attached greater importance. Leaving the defence of Karachi to be tackled only by one squadron of fighters and a half squadron of bombers was extremely unwise.

X. RE-ORGANIZATION OF AIR DEFENCE OF PAKISTAN

12. The subject of air defence has been discussed by us at some length in section (13) of Chapter VIII of Part IV of the Main Report. In the light of that discussion, we make the following recommendations: -

(a) Since it will not be possible for us to enlarge our Air Force to any appreciable extent in the near future, we strongly recommend that we should strengthen our air defence programmes by at least doubling our holdings of anti-craft guns by the end of 1972 and ultimately raising it under a phased programme to 342 Batteries as suggested by the Air Force.

(b) Efforts should also be made to procure ground to air missiles for a more effective air defence of the country.

(c) If ground-to-air missiles are not available, then efforts should also be made to get radar controlled medium HAA guns from China.

XI. Recommendations with Regard to Civil Defence Measures

13. This subject has also examined by us in Chapter VIII of Part IV of the Main Report, and we consider that the following measures are called for to improve the civil defence aspects in Pakistan: -

(a) The civil defence arrangements should be placed under the Ministry of Defence, and not be made the responsibility of the Ministry of Interior or other individual departments. The Central Government should accept the responsibility for the overall control and organization of the civil defence of the country, as Provincial Governments have not been able to shoulder this responsibility effectively in the past.

(b) Steps should be taken to improve the fire-fighting facilities in the country, particularly in ports and industrial areas.

(c) Industrialists keeping inflammable materials near lines of communications and other vulnerable points should be induce, or in fact obliged under the law, to accept responsibility for the protection of their materials, and make effective arrangements for fire-fighting in their establishments.

(d) Provision should be made for storing large quantitative of petrol and other fuels underground.

XII. Higher Direction of War

14. The deficiencies in the organization for the higher direction of war were examined by us in Chapter XI of Part IV of the Main Report, and in the light of that discussion, we proposed the following measures: -

(a) The three Service Headquarters should be located at one place along with the Ministry of Defence.

(b) The posts of Commander-in-Chiefs should be replaced by Chiefs of Staff of the respective services (This, we understand, has already been done by the Government)

(c) The Defence Committee of the Cabinet should be re-activated and it should be ensured that its meetings are held regularly. A positive direction should be added in its Charter to give the Cabinet Division the right to initiate proceedings for the convening of its meetings should be held even in the absence of the President or the Prime Minister under the Chairmanship of the senior most minister present.

(d) There should also be a Defence Ministers Committee and the Ministry of Defence should assume its rightful position as a policy-making body and incorporating policy, decisions into defence programmes after consultations with the three services. This should ensure the preparations of realistic plans for the national defence with in the agreed framework of (illegible) allocations. It should meet under the chairmanship of the Defence Minister and comprise the Defence Secretary, the three service chiefs, the financial adviser for defence, the Director General of Civil Defence, the Director General of munitions production, the Director General of Defence Procurement, the Director General of inter-services Intelligence Directorate, the Defence Scientific Adviser and any other Central Secretary or Service officer who may be required for a particular item on agenda. If the defence portfolio is held by the President or the Prime Minister then its meeting may be presided over by a Deputy Minister for or by the Minister in charge of Defence Production (illegible) Minister is available, the Defence Secretary should preside, irrespective of any considerations of protocol or (illegible)

(e) The Secretaries Coordination Committee as at present constituted, should continue

(f) (illegible) The three services should share (illegible) joint responsibility for national defence and that all plans and programmes for the development of the (illegible) forces should be based on joint (illegible) objectives, it is necessary. Therefore, that the three services Chief should (illegible) As Joint Chiefs of Staff and not merely as individual Heads of their respective Services. This Joint Chiefs or Staff should constitute a corporate body with collective responsibility having its own (illegible) staff for evolving joint plans and its own Headquarters located on one place. The (illegible) of chairman of this Joint Chiefs of Staff must be held by rotation, irrespective of the personal ranks enjoyed by the three service chiefs. The duration of the tenure should be one year at a time and the chairmanship should commence with the (illegible) Service, mainly, the Army. A detailed Chapter of duties for this Joint Chiefs of Staff has been suggested in Annexure 'I' of Chapter XI of Part IV of the Main report.

(g) Under the Joint Chiefs of Staff Organisation there will not only by a Secretariat but also a joint planning staff drawn from all the three Services. It might be designed as the Joint Secretariat and Planning Staff. It will be responsible not only for providing the necessary secretarial assistance (illegible) Also for evolving the joint defence plans and (illegible) studies of processing of all matters inter-(illegible) The Joint Chief of Staff may also have other Joint Common to assist them on such matters, as it may consider necessary.

(h) The weakness, in the (illegible) of the armed forces, which have been brought by light, (illegible) feel that there is need for an institution like the America (illegible) General which should be a body changed was the duty of carrying out surprise inspection and calling area the formations and (illegible) concerned to demonstrate that the (illegible) (this paragraph not readable)

(i) We have also felt the (illegible) for in Institute of Strategic Studies, preferably as a part of a University Programme. The need for such an (illegible) has been highlighted by the weakness in our joint strategic panning by the three Services. We are of the opinion that such an Institute will go a long way in producing studies of value for examination by the other defence organizations.

XIII National Security Council

15. Having examined the working of the National Security Council in Chapter XI of Part IV of the Main Report we are of the opinion that there is no need for super-(illegible) such an organization on the Directorate of Intelligence Bureau and the Directorate of Inter-Services Intelligence. The Security Council should therefore be abolished.

XIV. The Farman Ali incident

16. In view of the fresh evidence examined by us regarding the role of Maj. Gen. Farman Ali, which we have discussed in the concluding portion of Chapter III of Part V of the Supplementary Report, recommendation No. 7 made in the Main Report has now become (illegible); as we have found that in delivering a message to Mr. Paul Mare Henry, Assistant Secretary General of the United Nations. Maj. Gen. Farman Ali, acted under the instructions of the Governor of East Pakistan, who in turn had been authorised by the then President of Pakistan to make certain proposals for settlement in East Pakistan at the critical juncture.

ANNEXURE

THE SEQUENCE OF THE SIGNALS

We now propose to examine how the situation developed from the beginning of the war, i.e. the 21st November, 1971 till the surrender and it will be necessary for this purpose to quote extensively from the signals exchanged during the period between the relevant authorities for only then will it be possible to paint the full picture.

2. The first relevant signal is dated 21st November, 1971 numbered G-1104 from the Commander to the Chief of General Staff.

"from COMD for CGS one (.) as you must have noticed, IN-DIANS have aggressed and started attacking in strength along with rebels (.) fighting taken place in areas JESSORE, BHURANGAMARI, SYLHET, CHITTAGONG AND DAC-CA suburbs (.) JESSORE airfield shelled by INDIAN med guns (.) in view this pressure own razakars stated blowing up bridges and laying ambushes against own troops (.) two (.) highly grateful for having allotted additional infantry battalions (.) three (.) move programme for all elements very slow (.) time against us (.) therefore request move all battalions on emergency basis as done during war (.) new raising likely to take time therefore despatch battalions already raised (.) also since full DIV NOT being provided, provisions of two more infantry battalions raising total to ten battalions, squadron tanks, one BDE HQ extremely essential which be considered and despatched immediately (.) request confirm."

3. It will be seen that, right from the commencement, the note struck by the Commander is far from a happy one, although not quite as dismal as the later signals were. The picture given is of fighting having started in various areas and a demand is made for two more battalions, i.e. in addition to the 8 already promised him.

4. From the record of the signals we do not find any answer to this request; the next signal, that is on record is dated 22nd November and numbered G-1086 from the Chief of Staff to the Commander warning him that the enemy is aiming at capture of CHITTAGONG from land and sea and requiring him, therefore, "to reinforce defences CHITTAGONG area by pulling out troops from less important sectors as necessary."

5. One the 28th November, 1971 the Commander sent a signal in the following terms: "G-0866 (.) CONFD (.) for COMMANDER IN CHIEF from COMD (.) G-022, of 27 Oct. (.) most gratefully acknowledge your kind consideration in conveying highly inspiring appreciation at performance of our basic duty EASTERN COMMAND and myself (.) indeed indebted for great confidence that is reposed in us (.) nevertheless reassure you that all ranks by grace of ALL are in high morale and fine shape and imbued with true spirit of extreme sacrifice to zealously of defend the priceless honour, integrity and solidarity of our beloved PAKISTAN (.) rededicating at this critical juncture of our history I pledge on behalf of all ranks that we are at the

highest STATE of readiness to teach a lasting lesson to HINDUSTAN should they dare cast an evil eye on our sacred soil in any manner, may be through open aggression or otherwise (.) trusting in GOD and your kind guidance, the impactful and glorious history of our forefathers would INSHALLAH be fully revived. maintaining highest traditions of our army in case such a GRAND Opportunity afforded."

It will be noticed that at this stage the Commander not only expresses his determination to fight but even boasts of hoping to teach a lasting lesson to Hindustan and looks upon the coming events as a "grand opportunity afforded".

6. As we have noticed elsewhere the Indian intention to attack openly and .declare an all out war was not merely a possibility but a distinct anticipation of which the Commander had been forewarned much earlier, nevertheless, on the 5th, December, 1971 by message numbered G-0338 the Chief of Staff stated this clearly in the following terms:

"exclusive for COMMANDER from CHIEF OF STAFF (.) it is now evident from all sources including intelligence channels that INDIANS will shortly launch a full scale offensive against EAST PAKISTAN (.) mean total war (.) the time has therefore come when keeping in mind current situation you re-deploy your forces in accordance with your operational task (. such positioning would of course take into consideration areas of tactical, political and strategic importance we are all proud of our EASTERN COMMAND (.) well done." a clear command was thus given to the Commander to redeploy his forces in accordance with his operational tasks. The fact the message also talks of taking into consideration areas of tactical, political and strategic importance implies, we think, liberty to give up other territory if necessary. However, that has been made clearer later.

7. On the 5th December, 1971 again by message numbered G-0235 the Chief of Staff informed the Commander as follows:

"personal for COMMANDER from CHIEF OF STAFF (.) the enemy has stepped up pressure against you and is likely to increase it to maximum extent (.) he will attempt to capture EAST PAKISTAN as swiftly as possible and then shift maximum forces to face WEST PAKISTAN (.) this must NOT be allowed to happen (.) losing of some territory is insignificant but you must continue to concentrate on operational deployments in vital areas aiming at keeping the maximum enemy force involved in EAST PAKISTAN (.) every hope of CHINESE activities very soon (.) good luck and keep up your magnificent work against such heavy odds (.) may Allah bless you".

It will be noticed that now, at any rate, if not earlier, the question of territory had become of minor importance; far more material was now the defence of East Pakistan in the sense of continuing to occupy the bulk of it or, in the last resort, a vital part of it so as not to allow the occupation of East Pakistan by Indian forces to become a reality. It is characteristic of the methods of G.H.Q. at this juncture, however, that most unrealistically and even without any foundation, the hope of Chinese activities starting very soon is being held out. We cannot help observing that not only at this stage but elsewhere the GHQ held out vague or even fraudulent promises of foreign help. We are not detracting from General Niazi's share of responsibility when we say that GHQ on its own part also led him up to entertain expectations which could not possibly be fulfilled.

8. In answer the Commander on the 6th December, 1971 by a signal numbered G-1233 said:

"for MO DTE (.) special sitrep 4 (.) general comments (.) one (.) since 3 dec on start all out hostilities, intensity and weight enemy offensive in all fronts this theatre highly increased (.) enemy strength comprising eight divisions supported by four tank regiments, full compliment of support service elements in addition to 39 battalions BORDER SECURITY FORCE and 60-70 thousand trained rebels now fully committed (.) besides all enemy offensive supported by air (.) INDIAN AIR FORCE causing maximum damage 9.) have started using rockets and napalm against own defensive positions (.) internally rebels highly active, emboldened and causing maximum damage in all possible ways including cutting off lines means of communication (.) this including destruction of roads/bridges/rail ferries/boats etc. 9.) local populations also against us (.) lack of communications making it difficult to reinforce or replenish or readjust positions (.) CHITTAGONG likely to be cut off and thus depriving that line of communication also (.) additional INDIAN NAVY now seriously threatening this sea port with effective blockade of all river approaches (.) DINAJPUR, RANGPUR, SYLHET, MAULVI BAZAR, BRAHMANBARIA, LAKSHAM, CHANDPUR and JSSORE under heavy pressure (.) situation likely becoming critical (.) two (.) own troops already involved in active operations since last nine months and now committed to very intense battle (.) obviously they had NO rest or relief (.) due pitched battles fought since last 17 days own casualties rate both in men and material fairly increased 9.) absence of own tank, artillery and air support has further aggravated situation (.) defection of razakars/mujahids with arms also increased (.) none the less, in process defensive battle, own troops inflicted heavy casualties on enemy and caused maximum possible attrition on them(.) enemy thus paid heavy cost for each success in terms of ground (.) three (.) based on foregoing and current operations situation of formations this command now reaching pre-planned line of defensives (.) resorting to fortress/

strong point basis (.) enemy will be involved through all methods including unorthodox action will fight it out last man last round (.) four (.) request expedite actions vide your G-0235 of 5 Dec 71".

9. This is a fairly detailed statement of the situation and clearly now depicts a more pessimistic picture. there are passages, however, in this which we find it difficult to regard as being accurate. The statement, for example, that there had been pitched battles for the last 17 days with increased casualty rates is not really supported by the evidence which does not justify the statement either that heavy casualties had been inflicted on the enemy and maximum attrition caused to them. The last words in the message are significant but, of course, entirely natural since they asked for expedition of the action promised, namely that of Chinese activity. 10. On the same day desperately by message numbered G-1234 the Commander signalled to the Chief of Staff to inquire when the likely help was to come. 11. The next signal is from the Governor of East Pakistan to the President and before we quote the same it is necessary to state the circumstances we have now learnt from the evidence and which led to the message. A meeting had apparently taken place and a quotation from the statement of Major General Rao Farman Ali is worth reproduction: "On the evening of 6 December, Governor Malik asked me about the situation as he was receiving disturbing reports from all over the province. I suggested that he should visit the Corps HQ and get a direct briefing from Gen Niazi. Gen. Niazi briefed him. I did not accompany the Governor. On 7 December, after I returned from the Corps HQ morning briefing the Governor asked me to arrange for transportation for the ministers to go to their districts to mobilize public opinion. He said that Gen. Niazi had told him that the situation was under control and that the Corps could provide Helicopters to the ministers. (There were only four/five helicopters). I told him

that situation had perhaps changed a bit since yesterday and suggested if he could have another meeting with Gen. Niazi. Gen. Niazi came. He was in a terrible shape, haggard, obviously had no sleep. The chief Secretary Mr. Muzaffar Hussain was also present. The Governor had hardly said a few words when Gen. Niazi started crying loudly. I had to send the bearer out. The Governor got up from his chair, patted him and said a few consoling words . I also added a few words saying "your resources were limited. It is not your fault etc." We discussed the situation after he regained his poise. the governor suggested that an effort was required to be made to bring about a peaceful solution to the problem. After the conference I went out to see Gen. Niazi off. He said, in Urdu that the message may be sent for the Governor's House. "I agreed as I thought it was important for the morale of the troops to keep up the image of the Commander."

12. The account of the meeting is substantially corroborated by Mr. Muzaffar Hussain, the Chief secretary.

13. The message that the Governor then sent on the 7th December, 1971 numbered A-6905 is as follows:

"for PRESIDENT OF PAKISTAN (.) it is imperative that correct situation in EAST PAKISTAN is brought to your notice (.) I discussed with GEN. NIAZI who tells me that troops are fighting heroically but against heavy odds without adequate artillery and air support(.) rebels continue cutting their rear and losses in equipment and men very heavy and cannot be replaced (.) the front in EASTERN and WESTERN SECTOR has collapsed (.) loss of whole corridor EAST OF MEGHNA RIVER cannot be avoided (.) JESSORE has already fallen which will be a terrible blow to the morale of PRO-PAKISTAN elements (.) civil administration ineffective as they cannot do much without communication (.) food and other supplies running short as nothing can move from CHITTAGONG or within the province (.) even DACCA city will be without food after 7(?) days(.) without fuel and oil there will be complete paralysis of life (.) law and order situation in areas vacated by army pathetic as thousands of PRO-PAKISTAN elements being butchered by rebels (.) millions of non-BENGALIS and loyal elements are awaiting death (.) No amount of lip sympathy or even material help from world powers except direct physical intervention will help (.) If any of our friends is expected to help that should have an impact within the next 48 rptd 48 hours (.) If no help is expected I beseech you to negotiate so that a civilised and peaceful transfer takes place and millions of lives are saved and untold misery avoided (.) Is it worth sacrificing so much when the end seems inevitable (.) if help is coming we will fight on whatever consequences there may be (.) request be kept informed".

It must be conceded that this is a message which depicts a very grim picture indeed but we are unable to say that it was inaccurate. The statement that Dacca city itself would be without food after 7 days is not irreconcilable with what has been said by General Niazi that he had stocks to last much longer: General Niazi was thinking of perhaps, provision for troops while the Governor was thinking of the over-all position of Dacca. It is true also that there is an appeal in this message which questions whether it is worth sacrificing so much when the end appears inevitable, but the appeal is not for permission to surrender but for permission to negotiate a political settlement, of course, involving a civilised and peaceful transfer. General Niazi claims that this message issued without his concurrence, but we are entirely unable to agree that this was so. The evidence is that the message itself was shown to him and in any case, we are wholly unable to believe that Dr. Malik would have stated in this message that General Niazi said that he was fighting against heavy odds without adequate artillery and air support and, so far as the message talks of the military situation, he is expressly saying that he is depending on what General Niazi told him.

14. On the same day the Chief of Staff by his message numbered G-0908 informed the Commander that his message G-1234 quoted above in regard to the Chinese help was under consideration.

15. Also on the same day the Chief of General Staff sent a message numbered G-0907 which reads thus:

"for COMMANDER from CHIEF OF GENERAL STAFF (.) your G-1233 of 6 december refers (.) position as explained fully appreciated and the outstanding combat performance of all ranks is a matter of great pride (.) your tactical concept approved (.) hold positions tactically in strength without any territorial considerations including CHITTAGONG with a view to maintaining the entity of your force intact and inflicting maximum possible attrition in men and material on the enemy".

It is upon the words "your tactical concept approved" that General Niazi bases his claim of the approval of his tactical concept. This reference, however, is really to the Commander's signal already quoted of the 6th December, 1971 and numbered G-1233 in which he speaks of "reaching pre-planned lines of defence." It is not, therefore, a new approval that has been given, but implies an acceptance of the timing of withdrawing to these pre-planned lines.

16. The President also on that day sent a message to the Governor numbered A-4555 which is in response to the Governor's own message which we quoted above (No. A-6905) and read thus "from PRESIDENT for GOVERNOR (.) your flash signal number A-6905 dated 7 december refers (.) all possible steps are in hand (.) full scale and bitter war is going on in the WEST WING (.) world powers are very seriously attempting to bring about a cease-fire (.) the subject is being referred to the general assembly af-

ter persistent vetoes in the security council by the RUS-SIANS (.) a very high powered delegation is being rushed to NEW YORK (.) Please rest assured that I am fully alive to the terrible situation that you are facing (.) CHIEF OF STAFF is being directed by me to instruct GENERAL NI-AZI regarding the military strategy to be adopted (.) you on your part and your government should adopt strongest measures in the field of food rationing and curtailing supply of all essential items as on war footing to be able to last for maximum period of time and preventing a collapse 9.) GOD be with you (.) we are all praying".

This is characteristic of the kind of messages which the President has sent giving full but vague assurances. He talks of all possible steps being in hand and of world powers seriously attempting to bring about a cease-fire. He mentions efforts going on in the United Nations and gives advice as to food rationing.

17. On the 8th December, 1971 there are two messages from the Chief of Staff to the Commander numbered G-0910 and G-0912 which it is unnecessary to quote, but in regard to which it suffices to say that once again General Naizi was being told that actual territory was becoming of less and less importance.

18. The 9th December, 1971 was an important date by reason of exchange of several critical signals also. The first of these is No. G-1255 from the Commander to the Chief of Staff and reads thus:

"for CHIEF OF THE GENERAL STAFF from COMMAND-ER (.) one (.) regrouping readjustment is NOT possible due to enemy mastery of skies (.) population getting extremely hostile and providing all out help to enemy (.) NO move possible during night due intensive rebel ambushes (.) rebels guiding enemy through gaps and to rear (.) airfields damaged extensively, NO mission last three days and not possible in future (.) all jetties, ferries and river craft destroyed due enemy air action (.) bridges demolished by rebels even extrication most difficult (.) two (.) extensive damage to heavy weapons and equipment due enemy air action (.) troops fighting extremely well but stress and strain now telling hard (.) NOT slept for last 20 days (.) are under constant fire, air, artillery and tanks (.) three (.) situation extremely critical. We will go on fighting and do our best (.) four (.) request following (.) immediate strike all enemy air bases this theatre 9.) if possible reinforce airborne troops for protection DACCA".

We consider that no more hopeless a description could have been given from a Commander in an independent theatre to his distant Supreme Commander than this message was. Every possible element which would total up to a situation of utter helplessness is present in the message. Despite the fact that the Commander does say "we will go on fighting and do our best" we cannot be feel that these were empty words and the impression conveyed and intended to be conveyed was of an army on the verge of capitulation. The request for re-enforcement by airborne troops for the protection of Dacca was unreal for the Commander knew very well that even if troops were available the physical means of sending them to Dacca were not existent. The Dacca airfield was no longer useable and the Commander himself refers to enemy air action. In these circumstances we cannot believe that the Commander meant the request to be seriously taken. We are of the view that the request was deliberately put in for the purpose of providing an excuse for himself.

19. On the same day some nine hours later, clearly after having consulted General Niazi the Governor sent signal No. A-1660 to the President which reads thus:

"A-4660 of 091800 (.) for the PRESIDENT (.) military situation desperate (.) enemy is approaching FARIDPUR in the WEST and has closed up to the river MEGHNA in the

EAST by -passing our troops in COMILLA and LAKSHAM (.) CHANDPUR has fallen to the enemy thereby closing all river routes (.) enemy likely to be at the outskirts of DACCA any day if no outside help forthcoming (.) SECRETARY GENERAL UN'S representative in DACCA has proposed that DACCA CITY may be declared as an open city to save lives of civilians specially NON-BENGALIS (.) am favourably inclined to accept the offer (.) strongly recommend this be approved (.) GEN. NIAZI does not agree as he considers that his orders are to fight to the last and it would amount to giving up DACCA (.) this action may result in massacre of the whole army, WP police and all non-locals and loyal locals (.) there are no regular troops in reserve and once the enemy has crossed the GANGES or MEGHNA further resistance will be futile unless CHINA or USA intervenes today with a massive air and ground support (.) Once again urge you to consider immediate cease-fire and political settlement otherwise once INDIAN TROOPS are free from EAST WING in a few days even WEST WING will be in jeopardy (.) understand local population has welcomed INDIAN ARMY in captured areas and are providing maximum help to them (.) our troops are finding it impossible to withdraw and manoeuvre due to rebel activity (.) with this clear alignment sacrifice of WEST PAKISTAN is meaningless".

20. The President answered back immediately by his signal No. G-0001 which read thus: "from PRESIDENT to GOVERNOR Repeated to COMMANDER EASTERN COMMAND (.) your flash message A-4660 of 9 dec received and thoroughly understood (.) you have my permission to take decisions on your proposals to me (.) I have and am continuing to take all measures internationally but in view of our complete isolation from each other decision about EAST PAKISTAN I leave entirely to your good sense and judgement (.) I will approve of any decision you take and I am instructing GEN NIAZI simultaneously to accept your

decision and arrange things accordingly (.) whatever efforts you make in your decision to save senseless destruction of the kind of civilians you have mentioned in particular the safety of our armed forces, you may go ahead and ensure safety of armed forces by all political means that you will adopt with our opponent".

In view of what followed this is a very interesting response. In clear words General Mahya says "you have my permission to take decisions on your proposals to me". Although he says that he is continuing to take all measures internationally he leaves the decision about East Pakistan entirely to the Governor's good sense and judgement and undertakes in advance to approve of any such decision and also to instruct General Niazi to accept his decision. We cannot see how any interpretation can be placed on this message other than one of leaving the Governor entirely free to reach a political settlement.

21. Accordingly on the 10th December 1971 by message No. A-7107 the Governor informed the president what he had done. (By some clerical mistake two messages bear the same number A-7107 as is the case in respect of two other messages both of which bear the number G-0002):

"for PRESIDENT OF PAKISTAN (.) your G-0001 of 092300 DEC (>) as the responsibility of taking the final and fatal decision has been given to me I am handing over the following note to ASSISTANT SECRETARY GENERAL MR. PAUL MARK HENRY after your approval (.) note begins (.) it was never the intention of the armed forces of PAKISTAN to involve themselves in an all out war on the soil of EAST PAKISTAN (.) however a situation, arose which compelled the armed forces to take defensive action (.) the intention of the GOVERNMENT OF PAKISTAN was always to decide the issue in EAST PAKISTAN by means of a political solution for which negotiations were afoot (.) the armed force, have fought heroically against heavy odds and can still continue to do so but in order to avoid further bloodshed and less of innocent lives I am making the following proposals (.) as the conflict arose as a result of political causes, it must end with a political solution (.) I therefore having been authorised by the PRESIDENT OF PAKISTAN do hereby call upon the elected representatives of EAST PAKISTAN to arrange for the peaceful formation of the government in DACCA (.) in making this offer I feel duty bound to say the will of the people of EAST PAKISTAN would demand the immediate vacation of their land by the Indian forces as well (.) I therefore call upon the UNITED NATIONS to arrange for a peaceful transfer of power and request (.) one (.) an immediate cease-fire (.) two (.) repatriation with honour of the armed forces of PAKISTAN TO WEST PAKISTAN (.) three (.) repatriation of all WEST PAKISTAN personnel desirous of returning to WEST PAKISTAN (.) four (.) the safety of all persons settled in EAST PAKISTAN since 1947 (.) five (.) guarantee of no reprisals against any person in EAST PAKISTAN (.) in making this offer, I want to make it clear that this is a definite proposal for peaceful transfer of power (.) the question of surrender of the armed forces would not be considered and does not arise and if this proposal is not accepted the armed forces will continue to fight to the last man (.) note ends (.) GEN. NIAZI has been consulted and submits himself to your command."

22. We then come to the 9th December, 1971 on which date the well known message, which General Rao Farman Ali is alleged to have issued, was delivered to the Assistant Secretary of the United nations Mr. Paul Mark Henry. There is no denying that this message had a disastrous effect upon our stand in the United Nations; at that time it was thought, and it certainly was our impression also when we wrote the Main Report, that General Rao Farman Ali apparently issued this on his own. We are now convinced that this is not in fact so. He acted on the direction of the

Governor and with the concurrence of General Niazi. His own version of it, which in the light of all other evidence now available to us, we see no reason to doubt, is as follows:

"On 9 Dec. Asstt Secretary UN Mr Paul mark Henry saw the Governor. I was not present during their meeting. After the meeting and after he discussed it with Gen Niazi on telephone he initiated the signal A-1660 of 091800 hrs. a copy is attached at Anx 'C'. Main recommendation was: "Once again urge you to consider immediate cease-fire and political settlement". (The president's reply (below Anx 'C') was received at night. The Governor and the Chief Secretary discussed it. I was not present. They concluded that the responsibility to take the historic -decision was being placed on the shoulders of the Governor. I may add here that before the war a High Powered Committee had been established which could take decision acting as the Central Government under a situation where communication broke down between the Centre and Dacca. The Committee consisted of the Governor, Minister of Finance, Gen. Niazi, Chief Secretary and I was to be its member Secretary. The Chief Secretary drafted a signal (Anx'D') to the President with a copy to UN Secretary General. (The draft clearly shows that it is a civilian type message). I was asked by the Governor to take it to Gen. Niazi and get his approval for the step proposed. I along with the Chief Secretary went to Gen. Niazi. Present were Gen. Jamshed and Admiral Sharif. "After I had read out the proposals to UN. Gen Jamshed was the first one to speak with a enthusiastic response of: " That's it. This is the only course open now." Or words to that effect. Admiral Sharif Approved in Gen. Niazi asked in what capacity was the required to approve the proposed move. The chief Secretary said. "In your capacity as member of the High powered Committee." He gave his approval, I returned to the Governor House where I found the Governor and Mr. Paul Mark

Henry in my office (In my earlier report I had said that the Chief Secretary was also present. It was, perhaps, a case of misrecollection. The chief Secretary tells me now that though he had arranged for Mr. Paul Mark Henry to be at the Governor House he himself was not there). The Governor asked me to hand over a copy of the signal to Mr. Henry which I did. "The signal bore my signatures as it was to be transmitted though Army channels. Mr. Henry said that it will be discussed between Mr. Agha Shahi and the Secretary General and if M. Agha Shahi approved it will be taken up." It is true that this statement was counter-manded by the President but the damage that it could cause was done. With that aspect of the matter, however, we have already dealt in the Main Report.

23: Although this message is of the 10th and uses the words "I am handing over the note to Assistant Secretary General Mr. PAUL MARK HENRY after your approval" the note had been handed over on the 9th Clearly the Governor gave directions to General Farman Ali and, at the same time, dictated the message.

24. This completes the story of the note which was handed over to Mr. Paul Mark Henry and now it is clear not only that Major General Rao Farman Ali handed over his note with the Governor's approval but that the Governor himself acted under the belief that he was authorising it in turn with the President's approval. We consider it in the circumstances a wise settlement and indeed the only settlement which by this time was possibility of the proposal being treated a surrender for the expressly says that no such question will even be considered and that if his proposal is not accepted the armed forces will continue to fight to the last man.

25. We are, therefore, astonished to read the President's reaction to this message which he conveyed by his message of the same date No.G-0002 which reads thus:

"from PRESIDENT OF PAKISTAN (.) your flash message A-7/07 of 10 Dec(.) the proposed draft of your message his gene much beyond what you had suggested and I had approved(.) it gives the impression that you are talking on behalf of PAKISTAN when you have mentioned the subject of transfer of power, political solution and repatriation of troops from EAST TO WEST PAKISTAN(.) this virtually means the acceptance of an independent EAST PAKISTAN(.) the existing situation in your areas requires a limited action by you to end hostilities in EAST PAKISTAN (.) therefore suggest a draft which you are authorized to issue (.) quote(.) in view of complete sea and air blockade of EAST PAKISTAN by overwhelming INDIAN armed forces and the resultant senseless and indiscriminate bloodshed of civil population have introduced new dimensions to be situation in EAST PAKISTAN(.) the PRESENT OF PAKISTAN has authorised me to take whatever measures I may decide (.) I have therefore decided that although PAKISTAN armed forces have fought heroically against heavy odds and can still-continue to do so yet, in order to avoid further bloodshed and loss of innocent lives I am making the following proposals() one(.) an immediate cease-fire in EAST PAKISTAN to end hostility(.) two(.) guarantee of the safety of personnel settled in EAST PAKISTAN since 1947(.) three(.) guarantee of reprisals against any person on EAST PAKISTAN(.) four(.) I want to make it clear that this is definite proposal of ending all hostilities and the question of surrender of armed forces would not be considered and does not arise).) unquote(.) within this frame work you may make addition or ………………(blurred print)……..

26. That the President, in fact earlier, really authorised the Governor fully is indicated by the message of the Chief of Staff to the Commander of the 10th December, 1971 numbered (1-10237, the time of which is precisely the same s the President's own message. i.e. 7.10 P.M. and reads thus:

"for COMD from COS ARMY(.) PRESIDENTS signal message to GOVERNOR copy to you refers(.) PRESIDENT has left the decision to the GOVERNOR in close consultation with you (.) as no signal can correctly covey the degree of seriousness of the situation I can only leave it to you to take the correct decision on the spot(.) it is however, apparent that it is no only a question of time before the enemy with its great superiority in numbers and material and the active cooperation of rebels with dominate EAST PAKISTAN completely(.) meanwhile a lot of damage is being done to the civil population and the army is suffering heavy causalities(.() you will have to assess the value of fighting on if you can and weigh it against the heavy looses likely to be suffered both civil and military(.) based on this you should give your frank advice to the GOVERNOR who will give his final decision as delegated to him by the PRESIDENT(.) whenever you feel it is necessary to do so you should attempt to ...by maximum military equipment so hat it does not fall into enemy hands (.) keep me informed (.) ALLAH bless you."

It will be seen that the Chief of Staff re-affirms that the Governor will take the final decision. As the power to do so had been delegated to him by the President. We confess to a sense of bewilderment: so express are these messages from the President and his Chief of Staff that the President's repudiation of the Governor's decision is unexplainable.

27. On the 10th December also the Commander signaled to the Chief of Staff s follows: "from COMMANDER for CHIEF OF THE GENERAL STAFF(.) operational situation(.) one(.) all formations this command in every sector this under extreme pressure(.) brave(.) formations troops mostly isolated in fortresses which initially invested by enemy now under heavy attacks and may be liquidated due overcoming strength of enemy(.) Charlie(.) enemy possesses mastery of air and freedom to destroy all vehi-

cles at will and with full concentration of effort (.) delta(.) local population and rebels not only hostile but all out to destroy own troops in entire area(.) echo(.) all communication road river cut(.) two(.) orders to own troops issued to hold on last man last round which may NOT be too long due very prolonged operations and fighting troops totally tired(.) any way will be difficult to hold on when weapons ammunition also continue to be destroyed by the enemy rebels actions besides intense rate battle expenditure(.) three(.) submitted for information and advice."

The again is consistent with the situation so far reported. Indeed , now Commander admits that the orders that he had issued to his own troops to hold out to the last man and the last round may not be for too long and he asked for information and advice." 28. On the 11th December, 1971 the President sent another message to the Governor which is numbered G-0002 and reads thus:

"for GOVERNOR from PRESIDENT(.) do NOT repeat NOT take any action on my last message to you(.) very important diplomatic and military moves are taking place by our friends(.) is essential that we hold on for another thirty six hours at all costs(.) please also pass this message to GEN. NIAZI and GEN. FARMAN."

29. Presumably the order not to take any action on the last message refers to his message in which he gives directions for further proposals. It cannot be merely a repudiation of his earlier authorisation of the Governor for that had been already countermanded. It would seem by reason of the reference to General Rao Farman Ali that it had come to the notice of the President that it was General Rao Farman Ali who had handed over the note to the representative of the United Nations Secretary General. Plainly General Yahya Khan was hoping to retrieve he situation in the United Nations. It is to be remembered that Mr. Z.A. Bhutto then deputy Prime Minister designate, had already reached the

United Nations and found his hands tied. We do not enter into a detailed discussions of this aspect of the matter now s it has been adequately dealt with in the main Report.

30. Having been advised and even ordered to hold on for 36 hours at lest and also having been assured of intervention by friends on the 11th December the Commander sent signal No.G-127 to the Chief of staff in these terms:

"from COMMANDER FOR CHIEF OF STAF(.) enemy has helidropped approximately one brigade SOUTH OF NARSINDI and at 1630 hours dropped one PARA brigade in TANGAIL area(.) request friends arrive DACA by air first light 12 dec."

31. The Chief of Staff, no in answer to this message, but in response to earlier messages sent signal No.G0011 on the 11th December, 1971 to the Commander as follows:

"for COMMANDER FROM chief of staff(.) your no.G-1275 dec and PRESIDENTS message to GOVERNOR with a copy to you vide signal no.G-0002 of 110-130 December refer(.) one(.) for your personal information UNITED STATES SEVENTH FLEET will be very soon in position() also NEFA front has been activated by CHINESE although the INDIANS for obvious reasons have not announced it(.) two(.) very strong pressure internationally has been brought upon RUSSIA and INDIA by UNITED STATES(.) INDIA is therefore desperately in a hurry to take maximum possible action against you in EAST PASKISTAN to achieve a fait accompli before vents both political and military are against them (.) three(.) it is therefore all the more vital for you to hold out as the PRESIDENT had desired in his signal no.G-0002 o 10430 DEC (.) four(.) good luck to you."

On what basis the Chief of Staff was stating that the Unites State's Seventh Fleet would soon be in position and also that the NEFA front had been activated by Chinese we can not even conjecture.

32. The Commander's next message dated the 12th December, 1971 and numbered G-127 makes interesting reading:

"from COMD for COS(.) your G-0011 of 110245 dec(.) one(.) thanks for info and good wishes(.) two(.) vide my previous sig Comm 1 had issued orders to troops to fight out last man last round in their respective areas by estb fortresses(.) three(.) situation own doubtlessly extremely critical but will turn DACCA into fortress and tight it out till end."

As to fighting to the last man last round we have already seen his earlier signal but it is to be stressed that he now talks of turning Dacca into a fortress and fighting it out ill the end. Presumably in Dacca. The sudden change in the tone of the signal of 12th December and afterwards, appears to be the result of the COS signal G-0011 of 11th December informing "also NEFA front has been activated by Chinese etc."

33. The next signal is by the Commander on the 12th Dec ember, 1971 numbered G-1279:" from COMD for COS(.) one(.) of our officer taken PW sent to COMILA FORTRES by enemy with following messages(.) quote(.) if your all do not surrender we will HAND over all your prisoners to MUKTI-FAUJ for butchery(.) unquote(.) two(.) request immediately take up with world red cross authorities and C in C INDIA (.) matter serious."

It is interesting in the first place to notice that this was an unclassified .. and secondly to note that the only purpose of this signal was to complain of a threat that unless the Pakistan army surrendered prisoners would be handed over to the Mukti Fauj for butchering. As we think that this threat might have played some part in the final decision to surrender we merely take not of this for the present and will comment upon it later.

34. On the 13th December, 1971 the Commander sent message No.G-1282 which read thus: "For MO DTE(.) special situation report number 4(.) One(.) enemy(.) Alfa(.) build up at MATTARL SO 7344 by heliborne troops cont (.) enemy at MATTARL 7344 now advancing along road MATTAR-DMR RL 5624(.) bravo(.) details contact by para troop awaited (.) charlie(.) enemy cone also reported at DAUD-KANDI RL 7903 and two helicopters landed SOUTH OF NARAYANGAJ RL 5713(.) details awaited(.) delta(.) enemy making all out efforts to capture DACCA ASP(.) two(.) DACCA fortress defenses well organised and determined to fight it out." Of immediate interest to us is only the part which states that Dacca fortress defences are well organised and that the Commander is determined to fight it out. It may also be pointed out that the information of helicopters landing was incorrect.

35. On the same date he sent another message numbered G-1286 which reads thus: "from COMD for COS(.) one(.) alfa(.) fortresses in all sectors under heavy pressure(.) I am though with formations only n wireless(.) NO replenishment of even ammunition(.) bravo(.) DACCA under heavy pressure rebels have already surrounded by city and firing with RRS and mortars supported by IAF armed hels (.) INDIANS also advancing(.) situation serious(.) fortress defence organised and will fight it out(.) two(.) alfa(.) Promised assistance must take practical shape by 14 dec.(.) brvo(.) CHINESE fighting in NEFA will have NO effect(.) is effect can only be felt in SILLIGUR and by engaging enemy air bases around us." Obviously an even more grim situation is now reported and even Chinese fighting, the Commander asserts, will have no effect. Nevertheless, he re-affirming that the fortress defence is organised and that he will fight it out.

36. The need, however, for holding on for some time is stressed again by the Chief of Staff on the 14h December, 1971 by message numbered G-012 which reads:

"for COMMANDER from CHIEF OF STAFF(.) your G-1286 of 3 Dec.(.) the UNITED NATION SECRURITY COUNCIL. is in session and is most likely to order a cease-ire(.) knowing his the INDIANS ARE DOING all they can to capture DACCA and form a BANGLADESH GOVERNMENT before the cease-fire resolution is passed (.) as far as we can anticipate it is only a matter of hours(.) I need not therefore urge you to hold out till the United Nation Resolution is passed(.) I am saying this with full realization of the most critical situation that you and your command are facing so valiantly(.) ALLAH is with you."

The emphasis is on holding out until the United Nations Resolution is passed which, it is

anticipated, will being only a matter of hours.

37. Apparently this message was not clear to the Commander who by message No.G-1288 asked for clear instructions and upon this message there is an endorsement of the Private Secretary to the Chief of Staff as follows:

"Have spoken to commander Eastern Command at 0825 hours. He is now quite clear on the action to be taken. Have told him that Security Council is in session inspite of Russian veto. It is imperative that Dacca is held on at least till the decision is taken by the Security Council."

38. On the 14th December 1971 the President sent Signal No. G-0013 to the Governor and

General Niazi as follows:

"for GOVERNOR and GENERAL NIAZI from PRESIDENT(.) GOVERNOR'S flash message to me refers (.) you have fought a heroic battles against overwhelming odd(.) the nation is proud of you and the world full of admiration(.) I have done all that is humanly possible to find an acceptable solution to the problem(.) you have now reached a stage where further resistance is no longer HU-

MANLY possible nor will it serve any useful purpose(.) you should now take all necessary MEASURES TO STOP THE FIGHTING AND PRESERVE the lives of all armed forces personnel all those from WEST PAKISTAN and all loyal elements(.) meanwhile I have moved UN to urge INDIA to stop hostilities in EAST PAKISTAN forthwith and guarantee the safety of the armed forces and all other people who may be the likely target of miscreants."

The time given on the signal is 1332, i.e. 1.32 P.M. West Pakistan time. On the other hand the witnesses who were then in Dacca are unanimous that the message came at night. We have made all efforts to verify from the original and it is clear that the original does bear this time. Two circumstances moreover confirm that the time is correctly stated in the message. Signal No. G-0012, which we have quoted and which advises the Commander that the United Nations Security Council is in session, and, therefore, urges him to hold on was sent at 1235 A.M., i.e. West Pakistan time. Signal No. G-1288 from the Commander which asks that this signal be clarified is timed 8.45 A.M. (East Pakistan time) corresponding to 7.45 A.M. (West Pakistan time). On this last there in the endorsement which we have quoted and which speaks of the PS(C) to the Chief of Staff having spoken to the Commander at 8.25 A.M. West Pakistan time. Clearly these signals could not have been exchanged nor the conversation held to which this endorsement refers if the disputed time is 1.32 A.M. for obviously the commander would then say that neither the message nor the telephone conversations make any sense after the signal. We think, therefore, that the time is correctly mentioned on the message (signal G-0013) as 1.32 but are unable to explain the contradiction in the oral evidence.

39. We consider this is the most significant message of all the various messages that we have referred to and think it necessary to make some analysis of it. In the first place

it might be noticed that it is an unclassified message. i.e. it was sent in clear and was, therefore, capable of being listened to and, probably was listened to by India, as indeed by any other country. N itself and without reference to any other factor this alone must have had disastrous effect. The United Nations Security Council was in session, but it is difficult to see how we could with any confidence expect to secure any success there with this open confession of our weakness and clear willingness to accept any terms. Even those nations upon whose help we could have in some degree relied were hardly able to help after this.

40. Besides this important effect on Pakistan's case in the United Nation we think that it might we have prompted General Manekshaw to insist upon a surrender even though General Niazi was only proposing a cease-fire.

41. We have not been able to understand how such an important message came to be unclassified. Some mistake has occurred for it is both the duty of the Staff Officers ad that of the signal centre to ensure that some classification is given. The world "clear" although we have used it is not a classification used and when we have used it we mean only that bearing no classification it is , as we would put it in non-technical language, is clear.

42. The fact that it was unclassified also led to the feeling in the mind of those in Dacca that it might not be an authentic message but a hoax. Quite naturally, therefore, the Commander wanted to verify this and also to be sure whether this was meant to be surrender. It would be profitable to reproduced the following passage from General Niazi's written statement to us:

"This signal being unclassified was probably intercepted by the Indians in clear. As a first reaction we thought that it might be an Indian plant. However, I wanted to confirm its authenticity and also its implications:-

a. I was not fighting an independent war as commander of an independent army of a different country. I wanted to check about the overall GHO plan or cease-fire with India and is terms etc.

B. If I was to negotiate my independent ceasefire, I would not be from a position of strength.

It would tantamount to surrender.

Brigadier Janjua on request from my COS confirmed that this signal was meant to be UNCLAS on telephone. By about noon 14 December i.e. 9 hours after the receipt of the President's signal, I could get through to the CGS, Lt. Gen Gul Hassan Khan, and told him about the order of the President. He asked me as to what signal and what cease-fire or surrender I was talking about. When I explained to him he replied that he did not know about this order and since the President had issued these orders, I should talk to him and he then banged the telephone.

Earlier in the day, 14th December 1971, Governor A M Malik talked to me on telephone about the President's order. I told him that I had asked for clarification of the signal from the GHQ. He asked me whether I am going a agree to stopping the war or not. I replied him that I still had every intention to continue fighting. I heard about Governor's resignation in the afternoon and after strafing of the Government House same day he moved to Hotel Interconti-nental. With him moved him ministers and all civil and police officers. He wrote me a letter on the subject on 15th December as under:-

"My dear Niazi,

May I know if any action has been taken, from your side, on PAK ARMY Signal No.G-0013 dated 14-12-71 from the President to you and to me as the Governor. This message clearly said " you should take all necessary measures to stop the fighting and preserve the lives of all armed forces personnel, all those from West Pakistan and all loyal element." The signal also says "you have now reached a stage where further resistance is no longer humanly possible nor will it serve any useful purpose." Hostility is still continuing and loss of life and disaster continue. I request you to do he needful.

With regards.
Yours Sincerely,
A.M. Malice
Phone 25291-12"

43. It is a sad reflection on the state of affairs then prevailing at Rawalpindi, though in view of what we have said in the Main Report his can only be now a side light --, that at this critical juncture the Commander could not immediately get through on the telephone to the Chief of Staff, much less the President. The only person to whom he could speak immediately was Brigadier Janjua who, however, confirmed that the signal was meant to be unclassified. Not until about noon could the Commander speak even to the Chief of the General Staff who apparently did not even know what orders were being talked about. It does not seem that at any time the Commander could speak to the President himself and the highest hat he could reach was only the Chief of Staff and that not until the evening of the 14th and the Chief of Staff, according to General Niazi, merely sad "act accordingly" and the Air Commander-in-Chief, Ali Marshall M. Rahim Khan also insisted that the President's order be obeyed.

44. General Niazi has claimed both in view of the language of the message itself and of his subsequent conversations with officers at Rawalpindi that it amounted to an order to surrender.

For reasons which we shall elaborate a little later we are unable so to read it, but only as a permission to surrender. On the other hand, however, we are not impressed by the

134

contrary argument that it did not refer to a surrender at all, for this, we think, amounts to mere quibble on words. It is true that the actual world "surrender" has not been used, but it is expressly stated that further resistance is no longer humanly possible. This surely means surrender; at the most is might be interpreted to mean surrender on the best terms hat could be obtained, but, if necessary, unconditionally.

45. There follow some signals in regard to destruction of war material which it is not necessary for our present purposes to quote.

46. Where or not General Niazi understood this message as an order or permission to surrender he did convey through the American Counsel General o the Indians his request for cease-fire under the following conditions:

"a. Regrouping of Pakistan Armed Forces in designated areas to be mutually agreed upon between the commanders of the opposing forces.

b. To guarantee the safety of all military and para-military forces.

c. Safety o all those who settled in East Pakistan since 1947.

d. Not reprisals against those who helped the administrations since March, 1971.

47. In the meantime the Indians dropped by leaflets a message from General Manekshaw to General Rao Farman Ali Khan which reads thus:

"I have sent out two messages already but there has been no response from you so far. I was to repeat that further resistance is senseless and will mean deaths of many poor soldiers under your command quite unnecessarily.

I reiterate my guarantee of complete protection and just treatment under the Geneva Convention to all Military and Quasi-military personnel who surrender to my forces. Neither need you have any apprehension with regard to the forces of the Bangladesh as these are all under my command and the government of Bangladesh has issued instructions for the compliance with the provisions of the Geneva Convention.

My forces are now closing in and around DACCA and you (?)risons there are within the range of my Artillery, I have issued instructions to all my troops to afford complete protection to foreign nationals and all ethnic-minorities.

If should be the duty of all Commanders, to prevent the useless shedding of innocent blood, and I am therefore appealing to you once again to cooperate with me in ensuring that this human responsibility is fully discharged by all concerned.

Should you however, decide to continue to offer resistance may I strongly urge that you ensure that all civilians and foreign nationals are remove to a safe distance from the area of conflict. For the sake of your own men I hope you will not compel me to reduce your garrison with the use of force.

48. In response to General Niazi's proposal General Manekshaw sent a radio broadcast message to General Niazi, the gist of which was the he expected General Niazi to issue orders to cease-fire immediately and to surrender. In return he promised that they would be treated with dignity and consistently with the Geneva conventions and that he wounded would be looked after as the dead would be given proper burial. He also arranged for radio links between Calcutta and Dacca.

49. In response specifically to General Niazi's message General Manekshaw replied on the 15th December, 1971 as follows:

"Firstly, I have received your communications of cease-fire in Bangla Desh at 1430 hours today through the American Embassy at New Delhi.

Secondly, I had previously informed General Farman Ali in two messages that I would guarantee (A) he safety of all your military and para-military forces who surrender to me in Bangla Desh (B) complete protection to Foreign Nationals. Ethnic minorities and personnel of West Pakistan origin no matter who they may be. Since you have indicated your desire to stop tightening I expect you to issue orders to all forces under your command in Bangle Desh to cease-fire immediately and surrender to my advancing forces wherever they are located.

Thirdly, I give you my solemn assurance that personnel who surrender shall be treated with the dignity and respect that soldiers are entitled to an I shall abide by the provisions, of the Geneva Conventions. Further as you have many wounded I shall ensure that they are well cared for and your dead given proper burial. No one need have any fear for their safety, no matter where they come from. Nor shall there be any reprisals by forces operating under my command.

Fourthly, Immediately I receive a positive response from you I shall direct General Auroa the

Commander of Indian and Bangla Desh Forces in the Eastern Theatre to refrain from all air and ground actions against your forces. As a token of my good faith I have ordered that no air action shall take place over Dacca from 1700 hours today.

Fifthly, Assure you I have no desire to inflict unnecessary casualties on your troops as I abhor loss of human lives.

Should however you do not comply with what I have stated you will leave me with no other alternative but to resume my offensive with the utmost vigour at 0900 hours Indian standard time on 16th December.

Sixthly, In order to be able to discuss and finalise all matters quickly I have arranged for a Radio link on listening from 1700 hours Indian standard time today 15th December, The frequency will be 6605 (6605) KHZ by day and 3216(3216) KHZ by night. Call signs will be Cal(Calcutta) and DAC(Dacca). I would suggest you instruct your signallers to restore micro wave communications immediately().)"

50. It is to be noticed that the world "surrender" is for the first time used in these messages from India.

51. I here then follows a signal on the 15th December, 1971 numbered G-0015 from Chief of Staff to General Niazi as follows:

"for COMMANDER for CHIEF OF STAFF ARMY(.) your G-1310 of 15230 dec refers(.) I have seen your reply to the PRESIDENT and I have also heard over all INDIA RADIO GENERAL MANEKSHAW's reply to your message to him through UNITED STATES DIPLOMATIC channels(.) while I leave to you the decision I suggest that you accept the terms laid down by Chief of Staff INDIA as they appear to met your requirements (.) this is a purely local military decision and has NO repeat NO bearing on the political outcome which has to be decided separately(.) mutual decisions now arrived at by you will not be acceptable if repugnant to any UNITED NATIONS DECISION."

General Niazi asserts that although the Chief of Staff used the word "suggest" this amounted to an order. This might be true in general but in the peculiar context with which we are dealing we are not impressed by General Niazi's claim, for as we have said, he had been authorised and not ordered to surrender.

52. The reply of the Commander to the President to which reference is made in this signal is one dated 15th December and is as follows:

"G-1305(.) SECRET(.) from Command for PRESIDENT(.) your signal G-0013 14 December(.) I met AMERICAN Council General and gave him following in writing(.) quote(.) One(.) in order to save further hostilities in the major cities like DACCA I request you to arrange for an immediate cease-fire under the following conditions(.) ALFA(.) regrouping of PAKISTAN armed forces in designated areas to be mutually agreed upon between the commanders of the opposing forces(.) BRAVO(.) to guarantee the safety of all military and para military forces(.) Charlie(.) safety of all those who had settled in EAST PAKISTAN since 1947(.) TWO(.) on these conditions, the PAKISTAN armed forces and para military forces would immediately cease all military operations (.) THREE(.) I would further abide by any resolutions which the security council of the UNITED NATIONS may pass for the permanent settlement of the present dispute(.) FOUR(.) make this proposal with full authority vested in me by virtue o my position as martial law administrator of ZONE B (EAST PAKISTAN) and commander EASTERN COMMAND exercising final authority overall PAKISTAN military and paramilitary forces in this area(.) unquote(.) reply still awaited.

53. This completes the sequence of the message exchanged during the period immediately before the surrender.

www.ingramcontent.com/pod-product-compliance
Lightning Source LLC
Chambersburg PA
CBHW031552040426
42452CB00006B/282

Antonio & Mellida by John Marston

The first part. As it hath beene sundry times acted, by the children of Paules.

John Marston was born to John and Maria Marston née Guarsi, and baptised on October 7th, 1576 at Wardington, Oxfordshire.

Marston entered Brasenose College, Oxford in 1592 and earned his BA in 1594. By 1595, he was in London, living in the Middle Temple. His interests were in poetry and play writing, although his father's will of 1599 hopes that he would not further pursue such vanities.

His brief career in literature began with the fashionable genres of erotic epyllion and satire; erotic plays for boy actors to be performed before educated young men and members of the inns of court.

In 1598, he published 'The Metamorphosis of Pigmalion's Image and Certaine Satyres', a book of poetry. He also published 'The Scourge of Villanie', in 1598.

'Histriomastix' regarded as his first play was produced 1599. It's performance kicked off an episode in literary history known as the War of the Theatres; a literary feud between Marston, Jonson and Dekker that lasted until 1602.

However, the playwrights were later reconciled; Marston wrote a prefatory poem for Jonson's 'Sejanus' in 1605 and dedicated 'The Malcontent' to him.

Beyond this episode Marston's career continued to gather both strength, assets and followers. In 1603, he became a shareholder in the Children of Blackfriars company. He wrote and produced two plays with the company. The first was 'The Malcontent' in 1603, his most famous play. His second was 'The Dutch Courtesan', a satire on lust and hypocrisy, in 1604-5.

In 1605, he worked with George Chapman and Ben Jonson on 'Eastward Ho', a satire of popular taste and the vain imaginings of wealth to be found in the colony of Virginia.

Marston took the theatre world by surprise when he gave up writing plays in 1609 at the age of thirty-three. He sold his shares in the company of Blackfriars. His departure from the literary scene may have been because of further offence he gave to the king. The king suspended performances at Blackfriars and had Marston imprisoned.

On 24th September 1609 he was made a deacon and them a priest on 24th December 1609. In October 1616, Marston was assigned the living of Christchurch, Hampshire.

He died (accounts vary) on either the 24th or 25th June 1634 in London and was buried in the Middle Temple Church.

Index of Contents

DRAMATIS PERSONÆ
SCENE:—Venice and the Neighbourhood.
INDUCTION
THE PROLOGUE
THE FIRST PART OF ANTONIO AND MELLIDA
ACT I
SCENE I - Neighbourhood of Venice
ACT II
SCENE I - Palace of the Duke of Venice
ACT III
SCENE I - The Sea-shore
SCENE II - Palace of the Duke of Venice
ACT IV
SCENE I - Sea-shore near Venice
ACT V
SCENE I - Palace of the Duke of Venice
EPILOGUS
JOHN MARSTON – A SHORT BIOGRAPHY
JOHN MARSTON – A CONCISE BIBLIOGRAPHY

STORY OF THE PLAY

Andrugio, Duke of Genoa, being utterly defeated in a sea-fight by Piero Sforza, Duke of Venice, and banished by the Genoways, conceals himself, with Lucio (an old courtier) and a page, among the marshes round Venice. Piero proclaims throughout Italy that whoever brings the head of Andrugio or of Andrugio's son, Antonio (who is in love with Piero's daughter, Mellida), shall receive a reward of twenty thousand pistolets. Antonio disguises himself as an Amazon, and, obtaining an interview with Mellida, announces that her lover has been drowned at sea. The pretended Amazon is received as a guest in Piero's palace, and there quickly discovers himself to Mellida. Arrangements are made by the lovers to escape to England; but Piero gaining intelligence (through a letter that Mellida has dropped) of the intended flight, the plot is frustrated and Mellida escapes to the marshes in the disguise of a page. While Piero is giving orders for Antonio's arrest, a sailor rushes forward, pretending to be in hot pursuit of Antonio towards the marshes. The pursuer is Antonio himself, who had assumed the disguise of a sailor at the instance of Feliche, a high-minded gentleman of the Venetian court. Piero gives the pretended sailor his signet-ring that he may pass the watch and not be hindered in the pursuit. Arrived at the marshes, Antonio, distracted with grief for the fall of his father and for the loss of Mellida, flings himself prostrate on the ground. Presently Andrugio approaches with Lucio and the page, and a joyful meeting ensues between father and son. Andrugio and Lucio retire to a cave which they had fitted up as a dwelling, and Antonio, promising to quickly rejoin them, stays to hear a song from Andrugio's page. Meanwhile Mellida, disguised as a page, approaches unobserved, and hearing her name passionately pronounced, recognises the sailor as Antonio. She discovers herself to her lover, and after a brief colloquy despatches him across the marsh to observe whether any pursuers are in sight. Hardly has Antonio departed when Piero and his followers come up, and Mellida is drawn from a thicket where she had concealed herself. Piero hastens back to the court with his daughter, whom he resolves to marry out of hand to Galeatzo, son of the Duke of Florence. Antonio, returning in company with Andrugio and